8/30

DATE DUE

My
Marathon

Also by Frank Shorter

Olympic Gold (with Marc Bloom)
Frank Shorter's Running for Peak Performance

Also by John Brant

Duel in the Sun
14 Minutes (with Alberto Salazar)

My Marathon

Reflections on a Gold Medal Life

Frank Shorter

with *John Brant*

RODALE.

RODALE *wellness*

Live happy. Be healthy. Get inspired.

Sign up today to get exclusive access to our authors, exclusive bonuses, and the most authoritative, useful, and cutting-edge information on health, wellness, fitness, and living your life to the fullest.

Visit us online at RodaleWellness.com

Join us at RodaleWellness.com/Join

Rodale books may be purchased for business or promotional use or for special sales. For information, please write to:
Special Markets Department, Rodale Inc., 733 Third Avenue, New York, NY 10017.

Printed in the United States of America

Rodale Inc. makes every effort to use acid-free ♾, recycled paper ♻.

Book design by Joanna Williams

Library of Congress Cataloging-in-Publication Data

ISBN-13: 978–1–62336–724–4

Distributed to the trade by Macmillan

2   4   6   8   10   9   7   5   3   1   hardcover

RODALE.

We inspire health, healing, happiness, and love in the world. Starting with you.

To my brother Christopher John Shorter
1954–2015

Contents

Foreword

If ever there were a soul born and raised to cry out against injustice, it is Frank Shorter. If ever there were a soul who could completely channel his suffering into performance, it is Frank Shorter. If ever there were a soul who transformed his fame into unrelenting service to his nation, his sport, and humanity, it is Frank Shorter.

And if ever there were a soul who deserved to find peace, a peace beyond understanding, it is Frank Shorter.

In this brave book, he shows us that he finally has.

Frank has never been anything but brave. Four days after the massacre of eleven Israeli athletes at the 1972 Munich Olympics, Frank led me and Jack Bacheler to the start of the marathon. We were determined to show that barbarism only makes Olympians stronger. Our answer to the attack was to compress our anger and grief into our racing.

"This is as scared as I get," he said. "Now, let's go run."

Lord, did we run. Of course Frank won, I took fourth, and Jack ninth. That was the best finish by three runners from a single nation in history.

Frank's victory was so compelling that it inspired a huge boom in American running. He became a proud father to it.

Not much later we lost a great friend. Frank had helped Steve Prefontaine plan a risky, AAU-unsanctioned tour of track meets in Oregon for athletes from Finland and raced him in his final race, a 5,000 meters on May 30, 1975.

Four days later, on Hayward Field, Bill Bowerman, Frank, and I gave eulogies for Pre.

Bowerman, his college and Olympic coach, began, "Pre's desire burned to be the best, and he was. Step by step, as he matured, he reached his goals...He held every American record from 2,000 meters, two miles, through six miles and 10,000 meters. In 1976, his goal was Olympic champion and the world records related thereto."

Bowerman stopped and composed himself. He was the image of the wrongness of a father burying a son. I would never forget what he said next:

"He also burned with another great goal: *Emancipation*! Freedom for the US athlete... In the history of our sport, no one man had ever been permitted to bring a foreign athlete or team to the USA. The door was always locked by national red tape and dictatorship. Pre opened the door by persistence and difficult communication. You saw the Finnish athletes. Theirs was the first such visit this century...

"I pledge to Pre and call on everyone to join me. We invite all true sportsmen to fulfill his great dream, *freedom* to meet in international sport and friendship."

After's Pre's death and Bowerman's call, Frank was instrumental in what became a drumbeat of emancipation.

The Amateur Athletic Act of 1978, which Frank (a founding member of the USOC's Olympic Athletes Advisory Council) supported with all his heart, broke up the AAU, renamed it the Athletics Congress (TAC) and ensured athletes and coaches the rights and voices they had long fought for.

But under international rules, we still couldn't accept prize money and remain eligible for the Olympics. So Frank joined our runners' union, the Association of Road Racing Athletes, led by Don Kardong, who'd finished fourth in the 1976 Olympic marathon. ARRA created a professional circuit around the country.

The first showdown race was the 1981 Cascade Run-Off 15-K in Portland, Oregon. Nike put up $50,000 in prizes. And it was Frank who conveyed the situation to TAC executive director Ollan Cassell: Our pro league would succeed, and every good runner would be in ARRA and not TAC. If TAC and the IAAF didn't want to be obsolete tomorrow, they had to accept a deal where runners got paid but were not banned as pros.

The mechanism Shorter proposed was the trust fund. Prize money could go into accounts that TAC could monitor and say athletes were being paid for "training expenses." Cassell's acceptance of that deal ended a century of archaic amateurism.

We were free, free at last, to earn a living from running.

In 1976, Frank took the silver medal in the Montreal Olympic marathon, beaten by the unbelievably fresh Waldemar Cierpinski of East Germany. The memory moved Frank to become the first head of the United States Anti Doping Agency. And when the Stasi files were later unearthed, Cierpinski's name was listed prominent among the dopers.

"By speaking out on behalf of honest athletes who didn't have a platform and by establishing the framework for USADA," Frank writes, "I had done my best to lay that ghost to rest. I suspected that, for his part, Waldemar Cierpinski had never stopped looking back over *his* shoulder."

Frank's tough runner's psyche, his consistent training with the hardest intervals, his command of the pain of effort, all stemmed from the horrors of growing up in the family ruled by his father, in a 12-room house in Middletown, New York. Over the full arc of his life, he has contended every day with the damage his father did to him and his brothers and sisters.

"My father, Samuel Shorter, MD, known to his devoted patients as Dr. Sam," he writes, "lived an evil secret life in which he controlled his family through terror and out-of-control violence. It was so bad that I repressed most of his abuse and haven't been able to lash it together into a coherent narrative. Instead, shards of my childhood surface spontaneously, like icebergs bobbing in a calm sea. The only time he spent around us was to afflict us."

Frank never told me. He never told his first wife, Louise.

In 2008, his father died, and Frank was flooded by relief. Gradually, things he had suppressed began coming back up.

In 2010, giving a talk to delinquent, abused kids, with Bill Rodgers and Dick Beardsley, "fate was intervening," he writes, and it all poured out.

A little girl told him afterward that his story was her story, too.

Frank being Frank, he felt a growing responsibility to tell it more widely.

John Brant had heard about it from Beardsley and offered a trustworthy ear. Carefully, edgily, experiencing survivor's guilt because he couldn't help his sisters back then, Frank sat with Brant for two days.

The story was published in the October, 2011 issue of *Runners World*. Ever since, Frank has been working with Colorado's Healthy Learning Paths. He has always known that he himself has been a good father. But there, among the kids, he's found a peace in being welcomed with all the understanding of those who have survived hideous ones as well.

So, just as Frank helped to liberate so many athletes in so many ways over the years, this book has become his own emancipation proclamation. He strides forth freely, afresh, anew.

Kenny Moore
April 2016

Prologue

Riding My Pain

September 10, 1972. It was the morning of my marathon, and by every conceivable measure, I felt ready. The moment I rose from my mattress, and my bare feet touched the concrete floor of the balcony of our apartment in the athletes' village, I knew I was in rhythm. In balance. I didn't think I was going to win. I just felt confident that my plan would hold up.

My mantra: Ride my pain, work through the finish, don't get distracted. Don't think about the fact that, five days earlier, I had looked out from my balcony across the courtyard and seen a terrorist in a balaclava pointing an Uzi from a facing apartment window. Don't think about the 11 slain Israeli athletes, the air of stunned hysteria permeating Munich, or the chances of a follow-up attack. There would be time for that later. My job was to run—my trusted method for coping with chaos and managing mayhem.

I went into the apartment, keeping quiet so that I wouldn't disturb Dave Wottle and his wife, Jan. After Dave had won his gold medal in the 800 early in the Games, he celebrated by smuggling his bride into our unit. It wasn't much of a challenge. It was easy to forge an ID card or, as the Black September killers had proven, just climb the chain-link fence and push through an unlocked door. I had given Dave and Jan my half of a bedroom and dragged my mattress out to the balcony.

Now, I slipped on a pair of training shoes and headed out for a brief shakedown walk around the village, nodding to the heavily armed West German soldiers standing sentry, five days too late. Later, back at the apartment, I put on warm-ups and went down to the dining hall for my prerace meal ritual: toast, coffee, and fruit. There was plenty of time to digest before the 3 p.m. start. The afternoon post time suited me. I wasn't much for early mornings. Back home, I trained every day at 11:30 a.m. and 3:30 p.m. You could set your watch by my routine. Consistency, I had learned, was another way to tamp down terror.

I filled the next few hours by resting and reviewing my game plan. Earlier in the Games, I had finished fifth in the 10,000 meters. My 27:51:32 clocking was good for an American record but not good enough for a medal. After crossing the line, I stood for a moment, hands on hips, studying the times on the scoreboard. I might have looked disappointed, but in fact I was calibrating. None of my competitors in the marathon could touch my speed for a 10-K. This was good. My plan was falling into place. This was very good.

Over the course of my two weeks in Munich, I had made a point of running every section of the 26.2-mile marathon course. The previous Thursday I rode the metro out to the Nymphenburg Palace, at the 9-mile mark. I hopped off the car, took a quick glance at the graceful lawns and gardens and the imposing main building that had been built in the 1600s, and I made a note to return later as a tourist.

I then turned and ripped off a 3-mile time trial, mile 9 to mile

12 of the marathon course, the same stretch over which I planned to surge during the race. I covered the first mile in 4:30, then, over the next 2 miles, throttled back to a still-rapid 4:50 pace. It felt easy, almost preternaturally easy, only 75 to 80 percent of maximum perceived effort, the ease the product of the mass of searing speedwork I'd logged over the past few years. This was another favorable sign. After cooling down, I rode the metro back to the Olympic Village. Athletes received free public-transit passes for the duration of the Games, which, during those rigidly amateur years, seemed like quite the perk.

A few days later I took another metro ride, this one out to the military hospital where I had been born in 1947, when my father was serving in the newly partitioned West Germany as a physician for the occupying US Army. I liked telling people at the Olympics that I'd been born in Munich. It gave me a special connection to the city, and I hoped that visiting the hospital might provide an emotional boost in the final days before the marathon.

My field trip, however, proved anticlimactic. The military hospital turned out to be small and nondescript, resembling a clinic more than a hospital as we conceive of them in the United States. I tried to imagine my parents on the day of my birth—my mother's hair, my father's uniform—but came up empty. All I could envision were two amorphous, impersonal entities delivering me into the world. I realized that visiting the hospital had been a mistake. Any thought of my father was a mistake. I climbed back on the metro and rode home to the athletes' village.

Now, opening my eyes, I returned to marathon day. It was time to go to the stadium. I packed my gear, knowing that bottles of defizzed Coke had already been cached at the water stations along the course. Kenny Moore, my teammate on the Olympic Marathon team and my mentor for the event, had recommended Coke, with its restorative blend of sugar and caffeine, as the ideal midrace beverage. I shouldered my gear bag and went out into the day, which was shaping up to be warm and humid. I always liked running in the heat. For the past two years I'd been living and training in Gainesville, Florida, not far from the Everglades, one of the steamier places on the planet.

Kenny and I walked to the stadium together. I felt calm, but at the same time I felt something building. Just ride it like the Munich metro, I cautioned myself. Stand back from the tracks and step onto the car when it rolls up.

A few days earlier, we had gone to the stadium for the memorial service for the Israeli athletes. After the ceremony, Kenny said, "During the marathon, every step of the way, I'm going to be thinking about the victims."

"That's what those killers want," I said, "to get inside our heads."

Kenny went quiet for a moment. "How can you forget about all that's happened?" he said.

During the hundreds of miles we'd run together over the last few years, I had told Kenny just about everything about myself, but I hadn't talked about my father. "I'm not going to forget," I said. "I'm just not going to think about it."

A few minutes later, in the holding room in the bowels of the stadium, I sat with Kenny and Jack Bacheler. Jack was the third member of the US Marathon team, another training partner and close friend. Their presence lent a sense of normalcy to the proceedings. It might be the Olympics, but to us it was still just another track meet. The other medal favorites were on hand: Mamo Wolde of Ethiopia, the defending Olympic champion; Derek Clayton of Australia, the world-record holder at the marathon; and Ron Hill of Great Britain, who had run the fastest marathon thus far in 1972 and who had won that year's Boston Marathon.

Now it was time. We spilled out onto the track, into the bowl of the stadium. The lion's roar of the crowd washed over us. I flashed back to the 1970 US–USSR track meet in Leningrad during my second season of international competition. At the start of the 10,000 meters, I had glanced at one of the Soviet runners, read the letters "CCCP" (the Russian-language abbreviation for the Soviet Union) emblazoned on his singlet, and thought, *Yes, I'm really here; I'm in Russia*. I felt the same way now. *I'm really here, at the starting line of the Olympic Marathon.*

I glanced up at the press box and TV cameras. ABC was televising the race, with Jim McKay from *Wide World of Sports* calling the action and Erich Segal, author of *Love Story* and my former professor at Yale, adding color commentary. For a moment I wondered if my sisters and brothers would be tuning in back in Taos. Then I let that thought go and stepped to the line.

The gun cracked. Drawing on my track experience, I went out hard, breaking for position on the inside lane. At best that would save me a few meters of distance and a few seconds of time, but in the fraught late stages of a marathon, small early economies could pay big dividends. We circled the track one and a half times and then ran out of the stadium and onto the streets of Old Munich. We ran through Sendlinger Tor, an arched stone gate erected in the 14th century, and continued past the Bürgerbräukeller, where, in 1922, at the infamous Beer Hall Putsch, young Adolf Hitler spearheaded the rise of the Third Reich. We crossed the bridge spanning the Isar river, passed the massive Pinakothek art museum, and worked down the oak-lined paths of the English Garden. We threaded the needle through Siegestor gate and ran by the Odeonsplatz, a public square where Nazi mobs once massed.

I tucked into the lead pack, clicking along at a 5-minute-mile pace. It felt easy. Mile 5, mile 6, mile 7—just ride it, just read the room; that is, appraise my competition. Wolde, Clayton, and Hill; Kenny and Jack: They were all marking time, holding their places, thinking that the real racing wouldn't start for at least another hour. In 1972 the marathon was mostly a war of attrition. You ran at a steady pace and hoped that you fell apart a little later than the next guy. The previous December, at the Fukuoka Marathon in Japan, I had experimented with a new tactic, surging at around 14 miles and then easing back. I might try something similar here, the other guys thought, but not for a while. We were only at mile 9, the Nymphenburg Palace rising in front of us.

We left the road and entered the palace grounds. We ran past a fountain and approached a 150-degree turn to the right—a virtual U-turn. The pack slowed to negotiate the bend. That is, the other guys slowed; this was my moment. I cut out wide, to the left of the pack. As the other runners braked for the turn, I floored it, just as I'd rehearsed during my time trial the week before. I rocketed out of that turn like a rock flung from a slingshot, opening a lead that was 50 meters and growing.

My opponents were surprised but not impressed. I was shooting my bolt way too early, they thought. No way could I hold this lead, keep my pace, for 18 more miles. Wolde, Clayton, Hill, and the others were certain they would reel me in.

What those other guys didn't know was my capacity for riding my pain. I had been planning this move for an entire year. Or, by another way of reckoning, for my entire life.

1

Felix the Cat

In the spring of 2015, my younger brother Chris died. He was only 61 and had a masters in math and computer science, a very bright man. Of the 10 surviving children in our profoundly dysfunctional family, I looked most like my father—the same nose, the same thick mop of hair—and Chris, and possibly Nanette, my sister, resembled him most in terms of personality. Not the cruelty, of course, or the psychotic duplicity, but they shared a similar strain of stubbornness and combativeness. Chris fought back harder than the rest of us against our father's attacks and thus absorbed more punishment.

The beatings would go on for a long time with Chris. For the rest of us, not so long in real time, although in terms of psychic damage, the violence never ended. The beatings were relatively brief because my father would get tired. Pounding on a child was hard physical work. It would turn anaerobic in a hurry. He would curse and snort and sweat. We would be watching from the doorway of the victim's bedroom. For me, watching was worse than getting hit myself. Our father knew he had an audience. There was a strong element of theater to his sadistic performances.

They began downstairs in the kitchen late at night, after my father came home from rounds at the hospital, or after he had sat up with a woman in labor or cleaned and dressed the knife wound of a railroad worker injured in a barroom fight. After he had finished playing his role of savior of our town, he would come home, and the mask would drop away. Or maybe he just exchanged one mask for another. Maybe he never stopped playacting, even inside his own house. Even, perhaps, inside his own head.

Upstairs in our bedrooms, we would hear him interrogating our mother. By the timbre and volume of his voice, we could tell whether he'd been drinking—advantages and disadvantages, either way. He would grill her, asking about the day around the house with the kids. He wasn't trying to catch up on the news or reconnect with his family. He was fishing for a transgression, intent on uncovering a slight misstep that he'd conflate into a pretext for storming up the stairs, belt in hand, calling out the name of the night's victim. To justify his violence, my father needed to gin up a motive.

He didn't attack Chris more often than the rest of us, but my little brother's beatings stand out in my memory. Chris would thrash and flail. He would hold out a long time before he started to cry.

And now Chris was dying, from the complications of colon cancer. He had battled hard for several years, the familiar grinding cancer campaign. You pretend it will never happen to you, but it happens (it happened to me a few years ago, a pimple on the corner of my mouth blooming into a squamous skin cancer that required major reconstructive surgery). Chris's kidneys were shutting down, which messed up his blood-clotting mechanism, which meant that he was suffering internal hemorrhaging; bleeding to death inside his body. Now he was in the ICU at a hospital in Albuquerque,

New Mexico, and there wasn't much time. A few of his siblings had gathered—Ruth and Barbara and Mary and myself.

As we stood vigil, my sisters and I got to talking. We had rarely talked when we were kids, for the same reason that resistance fighters in Nazi-occupied countries avoided speaking to one another. Under torture, we didn't want to divulge information that would expose our comrades. That frightened silence basically continued into adulthood. We had no good times to remember, so we tried not to remember at all. But now we were aging; now our brother was dying. Buried crimes came to light. Splinters flew from our lifelong family train wreck.

My sister revealed that Sam Jr., our severely disturbed oldest brother, had sexually molested Chris when he was little, a behavior Sam had learned from our father, who had sexually molested my sisters when they were young. I remembered the time Sam Jr. threw a hatchet at me; the blade quivered in the wall above my bed. We remembered Chris getting hammered because he was stubborn, because he wouldn't back down to our father. No, my sisters and I agreed, there wasn't much good for the Shorter family to remember.

+ + +

My father, Samuel Shorter, MD, known to his devoted patients as Dr. Sam, lived an evil secret life in which he controlled his family through terror and out-of-control violence. It was so bad that I repressed most of his abuse and haven't been able to lash it together into a coherent narrative. Instead, shards of my childhood surface spontaneously, like icebergs bobbing in a calm sea. Dr. Sam: The only time he spent around us was to afflict us. The exceptions were so rare that they almost shine. I recall him playing with us in a swimming pool on one of our summer family trips. I remember him smiling on a chairlift in the Catskills or the Rockies—my father loved to ski.

My dominant image, however, even more indelible than the beatings, was his psychological abuse. The man was a master sadist, a dark genius. He could have taught the Gestapo or Stasi a trick or two. His verbal stilettos hurt worse than an actual truncheon.

I see him behind the wheel of our Buick station wagon, embarked on one of the house calls that formed a staple of his family practice back in the 1950s. Sometimes he would take me along, ostensibly to educate me, but, in fact, it was to terrorize me. I can hear him talking in a low monotone, telling lewd, horrible, racist, and misogynistic jokes, reciting the supposed sins and treacheries of my siblings, setting one child against the other.

Behind the closed windows of the station wagon, as he smiled and waved to the townspeople, he would keep spewing until we arrived at the house of his patient. Then, leaving me in the car to process his rant, he would transform into the prototype of a kindly family doc and go about saving the world. Very early on, I realized he was more of an actor than a physician.

A handsome, charming, diabolical actor. He was chunky and carried a bit of a gut, standing about 5'9" and weighing around 180 pounds. Even if I hadn't run marathons, I never would have let myself pack on the pounds, because I have lived my life by not emulating Dr. Samuel Shorter.

Another detail comes to mind: his tattoos. In the 1950s, it was odd for a professional man to sport tattoos, but Dr. Sam took pride in this common touch. One tat was straightforward: "Kitty," my mother's nickname, was engraved on his left forearm. On his right shoulder, ironically, he wore an image of the caduceus, underscored by the Hippocratic Oath: "First, Do No Harm." The tattoo on his right forearm was more difficult to interpret: an image of the cartoon character Felix the Cat. Did Dr. Sam identify with this character and his prowling tomcat proclivities? Did he regard himself as a hunter of the night? I don't know. I never cared enough to ask and hadn't remembered the tattoos until I saw Chris dying and started talking with my sisters. I specifically recalled Felix because I would see the cat's jaunty smile each time my father raised his hand to whip me.

The theater for our family's Gothic drama was Middletown, New York, 60 miles north of New York City, halfway between the Hudson and Delaware rivers in Orange County. This area was originally Iroquois Indian territory. As a boy I would often find arrowheads, or what I believed to be arrowheads, in a field by a creek where I caught tadpoles. In the 17th century, Dutch settlers sailed up the Hudson from their recently purchased Manhattan Island. The Dutch brutally eradicated the native people but failed to exorcise the valley's ghosts. This was Washington Irving country, the province of Ichabod Crane and the Headless Horseman. More than 300 years later, the old stone farmhouses dotting the countryside were still occupied by the descendants of those stern Calvinists; my boyhood friends had surnames like Van Orden and Van Fleet. The foursquare Dutch Colonial houses of our town were rumored to hold dark family secrets.

Fifteen miles from the Hudson River, at the midpoint of the Delaware and Hudson Canal, Middletown steadily prospered, becoming a nexus for the railroads running up to Lake Erie and its ports. Together, the New York, Ontario and Western (commonly known as the O&W) Railway and the Erie Railroad formed our town's economic engine. Good transportation promoted industry, and from the mid-19th century up until the time I grew up there in the 1950s and early '60s, Middletown hummed with furniture, shoe, and lawn mower factories. The town nestled comfortably and attractively in the heart of the Hudson River valley, anchored by the tall white steeples of the Presbyterian, Episcopal, and Catholic churches.

Our family belonged to the Middletown elite. Dr. Sam's father, my grandfather, was a prominent optometrist who was famous for his practice's catchy motto: "See Longer, See Shorter." My father graduated from Hobart College and married my mother, Katherine, his hometown sweetheart, who lived five doors down from the Shorters and who had attended William Smith College, Hobart's sister school. He graduated in 1942, in the midst of the Second World War, and the army sent him through an accelerated wartime program at Temple University School of Medicine in Philadelphia. He received his MD degree in 1945 and shipped out to Germany just as the war was ending. He was stationed at Wiesbaden, West Germany, near Munich, where I was born in 1947.

Later, my sisters, three of whom are nurses, would speculate that our father's psychopathology might have sprung from the searing cases and scenes he encountered as a young physician in Germany just after World War II and at the dawn of the cold war. Bavaria was a grim place then, with mountains of rubble in Munich, the region's bombed-out capital; massive displaced persons camps; and the Soviet army poised just a few miles to the east. But I don't think my father had it so bad. His practice at the big US Army hospital in Wiesbaden was mostly routine: setting broken bones, administering penicillin shots, and the like. In fact, he maneuvered to have my delivery in the hospital in Munich, where the army brass received their medical treatment.

No, I don't see Germany as the seat of my father's ferocity. A more likely primary source was my grandfather, the "See Longer, See Shorter" optometrist, whom I remember as a hard, dour man who never showed any affection for his grandchildren. My father

liked to tell a story from his own childhood. The family was driving on a trip to visit relatives in Missouri, his father at the wheel,
the kids in the back seat. One of the children let his teddy bear fly
out the window, which enraged the old man. Instead of stopping
the car and retrieving the teddy bear, he reached back and, without
taking his eyes off the road, raked the back of his hand across the
faces of all three kids in the back seat.

As he told this story, Dr. Sam appeared anything but trauma-
tized. In fact, he seemed delighted. My father was obviously
impressed by his own father's fluency and resourcefulness with
regard to violence. The sadistic streak clearly ran in the family.

In 1947, when I was an infant, Dr. Sam completed his military
stint and returned to America. Instead of rushing back home to
join the post-war prosperity flood of returning veterans, he chose
an alternative path. Just as there was no clear accounting for his
rage, there was no obvious source for my father's altruism, his
taking the Hippocratic Oath to an extreme, his overwhelming
desire to act as a savior in the world's eyes. He wasn't religiously
observant, nor did he express strong political convictions. Whatever its source, even if he only sought to compensate publicly for
his private atrocities, his drive to serve was daunting.

His first position in the States was serving coal miners and their
families in the heart of Appalachia, in a place called Ward Hollow,
West Virginia. We lived in a company house at the base of a desic-
cated mountain. Train tracks ran through our backyard, carrying
miners to the mine face. I remember my father showing me a .38
caliber handgun that he said he carried for protection from snakes.
What I recall most clearly, however, was receiving my first beating
from my father. Again, a shard, a fragment of a memory: I am
running, sobbing, across a hot asphalt road. I'm 3 years old. My
father has taken his belt to me because I've soiled my diaper.

After a year or two in West Virginia, Dr. Sam decided to return to Middletown to establish his practice and raise his family. The town was at its postwar peak, with factories churning at full employment and housing tracts sprouting. Babies arrived by the bushel, and Dr. Sam delivered a high percentage of them. He bought a grand, rambling Victorian home on Highland Avenue and ran his practice out of offices on the ground floor.

By all appearances, he was a brilliant and tireless young doc. He worked heroically during the 1952 polio epidemic, administering the Salk vaccine, the first wonder drug of the Baby Boom era. He set fractured bones and treated the measles. Even today his influence is remembered in Middletown. If you go to the public library downtown, Phyllis Nestor, one of the reference librarians, will recall that Dr. Sam treated her poison ivy. My friend Ed Diana, the county commissioner, remembers him as a pillar of the community. Ed proclaimed a day in my father's honor when he retired from the county health department in 1996.

But at home my father was a psychopath who inflicted extreme physical, emotional, and sexual violence on his wife and children. Just as he worked tirelessly at his profession, he worked tirelessly at hurting us. It was as if he'd taken graduate courses in how to break our spirit and mess with our minds. He berated one of my sisters for her crossed eyes, a condition he refused to have treated until she was 7. He never attended one of his children's games, races, performances, or recitals. He kept my mother as a virtual prisoner in her own house.

Highland Avenue was where the town's bankers and lawyers and doctors and their families lived their sober, industrious, orderly lives. The Clemson family, for instance, owned the eponymous lawn mower factory, Middletown's signature employer. Clemson manufactured the nation's finest push mowers. The company was our town's version of Kodak or General Motors, its ascendance as seemingly eternal as the lawns of America sprouting every spring. Our house, the Shorter house, stood just down the avenue from the mansion that the Clemson family donated for use as the Middletown YMCA.

We had more than a dozen rooms, a mansard roof, and a big wraparound porch. The house commanded a sweeping view of the town below. My father's medical office on the ground floor had a separate entrance. He worked late and typically slept late in the mornings, not rising until after we had left for school. We rarely saw him—he never sat down to dinner with us except on major holidays—but we were constantly aware of him. The central theme of my boyhood, the ambient light behind the pulsing of isolated memories: eternal vigilance, constantly monitoring my father's whereabouts, anticipating his moods, hustling to stay either out of his way or one step ahead of him, seeking not to anger him or commit any infraction that he could distort into a motive for punishment. The constant threat of his anger, the lingering air of menace, was more draining than his actual beatings.

The beatings happened at night, when our neighbors couldn't see or hear them, and Dr. Sam drew on his professional expertise so as not to leave scars that townspeople could discover in the light of day. (Since our father was also our pediatrician, he didn't worry about a colleague discovering the evidence.) If only we had had smartphones then, with a button to surreptitiously push to audibly record our father's grunts and visibly chronicle the lash of his belt. But there were no smartphones, and he got away with his crimes. At 5 years of age, my sister had scars on her groin with the outline of my father's belt buckle. Another sister cried because her favorite long-sleeved sweater rubbed painfully against the open welts on her shoulders. A third sister was ashamed to shower during middle school gym class, lest her teacher see the purple bruises running up and down her back.

Our mother couldn't offer much protection. Katherine was intelligent and refined, a good pianist and a very good painter, talented enough to be recognized by professionals and win competitions. My father discouraged her music because there was the threat of her going outside the house with it or of her inviting other musicians into our home. Painting kept her locked away in her attic studio, across the hallway from my bedroom. All of us lived under my father's thumb, but the thumb ground down hardest on our mother. She bore 12 children and seemed perpetually pregnant, and in between full-term deliveries she suffered a number of miscarriages. More than once, I recall her being hauled away in an ambulance.

Over time, my mother devolved into a virtual hermit who rarely left the house. "Whenever I left you children alone with your father, something bad would happen," she told me when I was grown. At age 9, I started doing the family grocery shopping, pulling a red wagon up and down the hill behind our house. In December I would haul in a Christmas tree and put it up and decorate it. Later, as a teenager, I made sure to keep the cars filled with gas because even a half-empty tank would enrage Dr. Sam.

Sam Jr. was the eldest of the kids, but due to his emotional instability, I served as the de facto number-one son, which further complicated relations with my father. In general, Dr. Sam felt threatened by me and constantly tried to undermine me. At the same time he drew reflected glory from my achievements and sought to enlist me as his ally. When I rode with him on those gruesome house calls, he would by turns criticize my sisters and brothers, trying to set me against them to patronize me. The kind courtly doc, whom all the women in town adored and held up as a gentlemanly paradigm to their husbands, would regale me within the confines of our station wagon with the most loathsome sexist comments and jokes. By his lights, women were no more than holes, although he used a more explicit term. I was 9 years old, listening to this spew.

Once on Thanksgiving night he dragged me away from the dinner table to accompany him to the emergency room at the local hospital. My father always volunteered to be on call during weekends and holidays, which endeared him to his colleagues, and gave us, his kids, another reason to remain silent about his crimes: Given the man's proven generosity and selflessness, who in town could possibly believe our stories? How could we fully believe them ourselves?

I was perhaps 10 or 11 that Thanksgiving. The phone rang— my father was needed at the hospital. As he grabbed his coat, he told me to come along with him. Did he know what he was doing or was he improvising the whole while? Even today I couldn't tell you. At the emergency room we were greeted by a grotesque sight—a man's skull had been split open in a drunken brawl. Amazingly, the man was still conscious. My father did what he could and called for a surgeon. Then, in front of the patient, he summoned me into the treatment room. He held a piece of viscera to my face. "See this?" he said. "This is a piece of brain."

He wasn't trying to educate; he was trying to humiliate his patient and traumatize his son. Of course he succeeded but only to a degree. By that point I was already countering my father, unconsciously building a defense and casting about for an escape route.

I can't explain why I survived relatively intact, while my mother and siblings, in their various styles and to varying degrees, suffered. My rebellion was never stated or overt. I wasn't as brave as Chris was, and the attacks I suffered were never as brutal and soul killing as those inflicted on my sisters. I made the decision very early on to live my life by a single guiding principle: I would not become like my father; I would not prolong the violence; I would not play into his game.

Because he wanted us to live in fear, I refused to live in fear. Because he wanted to control our every thought and action, for us to always be aware of him, I blotted the man from my mind as soon as I walked out the door on Highland Avenue. At school I didn't worry about what was waiting for me at home. I didn't think about home until I walked back through the door, at which point I'd start plotting escape routes and diversionary tactics for my siblings and myself. Away from the house, I tried not to burden myself with "what ifs." Instead, I got ready. I made a plan and watched to see how it would turn out. Which is pretty much how I approached my marathons, and pretty much the way I still live today.

But not thinking, not worrying, and not fearing could only take me so far. I positively dealt with my predicament by moving. Baseball, football, swimming at the Y, cycling around town, walking to and from school, tearing around the playground: As long as I was moving, my brain and heart stayed even. It was hell to be pinned down—in the station wagon during Dr. Sam's house calls, in bed when he mounted the stairs at night. The way I dealt with stress was through movement. From the outside it appeared like the healthy free-ranging activity of an energetic small-town boy in Eisenhower-era America. But in fact, fear and desperation drove me.

My friends' homes formed another refuge. Foremost among them were the Prestons; my best friend, Alec Preston, and his wonderful parents, Dr. Alex Preston, an esteemed general surgeon, and his equally terrific mother, Mary Heard Preston, who was responsible for having the town's low-income housing built, and from her position on the school board established one of the nation's first talented-and-gifted programs, the track I followed from middle school until the day I went away to boarding school. Even if they'd been less distinguished, I would have cherished my time spent in their household simply because the Prestons were a loving, functional family. They projected an air of mutual respect and affection that was the opposite of the atmosphere in my home. Other sources of hope were people like Mr. Parmalee, the YMCA director. There was nothing special about Mr. Parmalee. He just liked kids and loved his job. Being around the man made me feel happy.

I drew strength from these people. They never knew how much they meant to me. I never breathed a word to them about the situation at home. The Prestons never suspected anything dark about Dr. Sam. Dr. Preston always praised my father, saying he was such a fine physician. But always, inevitably, I had to depart the Preston house or the Y and return to the house on Highland Avenue.

Home was bearable, however, because my father wouldn't be there. He would still be working, busy either with house calls or at the hospital or down in his office. We ate dinner in peace and usually in silence. We did our homework, putting off going to bed. During my early years I shared a bedroom with Sam Jr., who was 18 months older. I was almost as frightened of him as I was of my father. After he threw that hatchet at me, I just tried to stay as far away from my big brother as possible.

No matter how soundly I slept, I always heard my father when he came in after finishing work. I listened to him cross-examine my mother downstairs in the kitchen—his increasingly strident questions and her increasingly frantic demurrals: *No, it wasn't like that; he didn't do it on purpose. . . .* But by then it was already too late.

I heard his footsteps on the stairs and listened to him sounding our names as he decided which of us he was going to wallop. I tensed and waited. Then the door flew open, and my father stood framed by the light of the hallway. When he came at me, it was almost a relief; it was easier to get hammered myself than to watch one of my siblings suffer. He pounced like a grizzly bear mauling a camper, pulling me out of bed and tearing away my pajamas to expose my bottom. I could smell the whiskey on his breath, which was both good news and bad. Alcohol would juice his rage, but if he was sufficiently loaded, he might fumble around and use the strap end of his belt instead of the buckle.

Usually he found the buckle. Seizing me with his left hand, he applied the belt with the right. He would hit me so hard that he grunted like a power lifter; I can still hear the uh-huhh of his voice as he got his weight behind each blow. He would hit me with such anger, hatred, and pent-up rage that I almost felt sorry for him. Even as he administered the blows, I recognized, in some small, still sector of my mind, that I wasn't responsible for them. Nothing outside of his own sick mind could possibly elicit this outrage.

My father would whip me until his strength gave out. If I wept too loudly, he would mutter the bully's cliché: Quit your blubbering or I'll really give you something to cry about. So I tried my best not to cry. I isolated my pain in a place where I could watch and control it. Finally he'd tire from the effort—he really put a lot of energy into his attacks—and, again like a grizzly bear, huff out of my bedroom.

In the morning I would cover my bruises beneath my clothes, eat a quick breakfast, keeping very quiet so as not to disturb the beast playing the role of my father, who slept upstairs. And then, obliterating Dr. Sam from my consciousness, I headed out into my All-American Middletown day. I did well in school, earning good grades without drawing the ire of other kids for being the high-achieving doctor's son. Perhaps I had my father to thank for my acceptance; he was the kindly, enormously popular doc who made house calls when the kids were down with measles or chickenpox and "forgot" to send bills to financially struggling patients.

Also due to my father's negative example, I detested bullying in any form, avoided cliques, and disliked manifestations of privilege. I made friends from all the castes and classes in Middletown, from the Van Ordens of Highland Avenue to the Testas of the Italian-American neighborhood. I was a decent but unexceptional athlete, playing a solid first base on my Little League team and rising to the top of the ping-pong ladder at the Y: the slight, modestly talented kid who was always hustling. I also loved to ski, the one unalloyed gift I received from Dr. Sam. The only time I saw him relaxed and happy was on a mountain.

As I grew older, reaching the upper elementary school years, my father's psychological manipulation and bullying continued, and the atmosphere around the house grew increasingly toxic. But Dr. Sam stopped physically beating me. I was now old enough to resist his attacks, so in cowardly fashion he turned his belt toward the younger children. As I completed fifth grade—I was 11 or so at this point—my mother tried to get Sam Jr. out of the house; it was time to do something with him before it was too late.

My older brother likely suffered from severe emotional and learning problems. He struggled to make friends and was often violent and predatory toward his younger siblings. Perhaps because he was his firstborn namesake, my father never beat my older brother, and I don't remember Dr. Sam criticizing him as he did my other sisters and brothers. Criticism was unnecessary; the damage he inflicted on Sam Jr. was more direct and permanent. In a last-ditch attempt to reclaim Sam Jr. and get him out of the house, my mother arranged for him to audition for a spot at The Cathedral School of St. John the Divine Choir in New York City.

How my mother chose singing as an escape route for my brother, I have no idea. He evidenced no talent for music. And why she picked St. John the Divine, one of the top schools of its kind, is another mystery. Probably someone in the Preston circle provided a contact. Whatever the provenance for this unlikely mission, my mother and brother traveled down to Manhattan for the audition, and I went along for the ride.

I don't recall many details of that day, just that my brother bombed, as he must have known he would, and that afterward the director, hoping to salve my mother's disappointment, offered to give me an audition. I can't remember what piece I sang, just that my soprano voice was of sufficient promise for the director to offer me a slot at the prestigious school. My mother eagerly accepted the offer. I was up for the adventure (my brother was likely relieved that I and not he would have to endure the torture), and so I spent my sixth grade year in a choir boarding school in New York City.

It was a curious, mostly pleasant year. While I was relieved to get out of the house and away from my father, I missed my siblings and friends in Middletown; my baseball, swimming, and ping-pong; and the approbation of my teachers. While I enjoyed singing and competently filled my role in the choir, it was clear I had no gift for music. What I mostly remember was excelling during field day—most of the students were indoor types, clumsy at games—and comforting the younger children through their bouts of home-sickness. St. John the Divine drew students from around the country and from some foreign nations, and the kids rarely saw their parents. You could hear them crying at night. Since I didn't suffer those kinds of blues, I assumed the role of cheerful older brother. Thus the year passed. At the end of sixth grade, I called it quits on serious singing (although I would later join a singing group in college) and returned to Middletown.

I had gone down to New York as an 11-year-old boy and returned as a rising seventh grader on the edge of adolescence. I was too big to hammer any longer, and I was eager to spread my wings. At the same time I was still a boy, with a juvenile's imagination and penchant for daydreaming. I developed a fascination with ski racing. I had positive associations with skiing due to my father's enjoyment of the sport, and Alpine racing was beginning to appear on TV shows like ABC's *Wide World of Sports*.

In dark, wintry Middletown, watching the racers flash down the sunny Alpine slopes, with gorgeous European girls admiring them, I thought the sport seemed the height of glamour. I resolved to become one of those gleaming daredevils. I read in a ski magazine that the French racers trained in the off-season by running the roads. I was home for the summer and needed an outlet for my energy and a reason to get out of the house. Why not give running a try?

I laced up my PF Flyers and set out from the house, choosing as my destination Veraldi Junior High School, where I would start the seventh grade that September. In the summer of 1959, nobody ran in a place like Middletown. The high school track athletes didn't even train during the off-season. It was a novel idea, so novel that I'm sure no one noticed me running across town in my white gym shorts. No one took me seriously. I was just a skinny little boy, Dr. Sam's son, who must have been late for the movies or baseball practice.

2

The House on Highland Avenue

From the first step, I loved running. For years I'd been moving to work off my fear and stress—cycling and swimming and playing sandlot football and diving for ground balls as a Little League first baseman. But here, with running, there was motion concentrated, motion in its purest, most elemental and powerful form. It required neither teammates nor equipment and conformed to no rules or structure. I just had to roll out the front door on Highland Avenue, cut over to Wickham Avenue, and work my way under the shade trees along the quiet blocks of houses set well back from the sidewalk, arriving sweating and avid at the fieldstone school building 2.3 miles away.

I loved running but didn't think about it much; I didn't assume it would take me anywhere but school. I didn't try to go faster, and that summer I didn't even run systematically, going out at various times of day and not worrying if I missed a day or even a week of running. I ran in a pair of low-top canvas sneakers with flexible rubber soles. The common running shoe, now worn by millions around the world, hadn't been invented yet. I had no role model. I received no encouragement but no discouragement either. The chief reaction to my running, when there was any reaction at all, was a sort of bemused bafflement.

One summer day I set out on a route that carried me a few miles through town, traversed Davidge Park (a street through the park has since been named Frank Shorter Way), and ended at the Preston house, where I was greeted as if I were a member of the family. I could take a shower, or at least hose down in the yard, and sit in the shade by their tennis court while Mrs. Preston fed me a snack and poured a tall glass of lemonade. One day, as I sat there sweating and gulping, Mrs. Preston, who like just about everybody in those days equated running with punishment, asked me, "Frank dear, why are you doing this to yourself?"

All I could say was that I liked it, and that was explanation enough for Mrs. Preston. It was certainly more than my own mother or father ever had asked of me. Finally it was time to leave the Prestons' and go home. I would draw out the trip to delay my arrival, making loops and detours among the streets of Middletown. I was in no hurry to leave the streets on which I found release and solace and the house where I was respected and cared for to return home, where the opposite of solace and respect awaited.

The summer ended, the school year started, and I embarked on my plan to run back and forth to school. I would leave the house at the same time each morning, but before long I found myself arriving at school with minutes to spare. The junior high had a dress code at the time, only lace-up leather shoes were permitted, but I talked our principal into making an exception in my case and proudly wore my low-cut canvas sneakers in class.

I was getting better at running but still didn't think it was important in and of itself. It was just something I did. I wasn't even adamant about running every day. If the opportunity presented, I would accept a ride. Some mornings I stopped off at the house of my friend Maury Strauss. I would wait for Maury to finish his piano lesson, and if the lesson ran late, his mother would drive us to school.

But most mornings I ran. When I ran, always carrying my books in the crook of my left arm, I could forget what was happening at home, and at school I began to forge an identity as a runner. I must have seemed eccentric, but my peers always respected me. I talked our gym teacher into letting me run laps during PE class, while the other guys played flag football.

So passed my junior high years. I didn't regard running as a means to an end; instead, it was a way to relieve stress, which if anything, had intensified. Life continued the same on Highland Avenue. My father inflicted his violence while continuing to present a saintlike persona to the community. As the de facto eldest son, I became the protector for my mother and younger siblings. By now I was an expert on reading Dr. Sam's moods and predilections.

There wasn't much you could do once his rage was ignited. Once he started climbing the stairs at night, there was no stopping him. So I focused on preventing his anger from building. I kept out of his way and made sure my sisters and brothers did the same. When he went on the prowl for a child to accompany him on those excruciating house calls, I would clear out the house. When I went grocery shopping, I always bought the snacks and treats that he favored. I kept a close eye on the conduct of my sisters, who, as they approached their own adolescent years, presented as sexual prey to my father.

"He raped me when I was 14 years old," my sister Nanette says. "I came home from a date, and he said I was 5 minutes past curfew. He called me terrible names. He started to whip me as punishment, and the whipping turned into something else. He said he would kill me if I ever breathed a word about this, and I believed him. It changed my life forever. He used sexual abuse as part of his overall scheme of domination and fear. It was part of his sick purpose to keep us under his thumb."

I was just coming to my own maturity, trying to make sense of my own urges and impulses. I was vaguely aware of something going on with my father and sisters but didn't know for sure. My sisters were too petrified to talk about it, and even if they could have brought themselves to talk, they didn't have the vocabulary for expressing what had been done to them. The awareness and resources that we take for granted today weren't available then. We kept it all inside—inside the house, inside ourselves. I didn't learn the full truth about the rapes and sexual abuse until I was middle-aged and finally went public about my father's crimes.

To a certain degree I succeeded in diverting or blunting Dr. Sam's attacks. But some nights my father would still mount the stairs, calling out the name of one of my sisters or brothers. I would beg and plead with him to stop. I would pull at his arm, but he would swat me away. My inability to protect my sisters and brothers drilled me to my core. I coped by repressing the images, impressions, and memories and by running.

During my morning run to school, I was able to dispel the physical and psychic poisons, discharge some of the guilt, and start my public day with a clean slate—clean, that is, on the outside. I cherished the time I spent in my friends' homes and never hosted them in my own house.

My father continued to stride our community as a healer and hero, and Middletown continued to steam along as a model of midcentury American prosperity, with the lawn mower and furniture factories humming at full capacity; the trains running on time; the downtown department stores, lunch counters, and haberdashers doing a brisk business; and the first commuting suburbanites starting to move up from New York City. I assumed I would continue to play my familiar schizoid role in the secret Shorter psychodrama, but then something happened to change the script.

3

Pie Race

My mother had failed once to get Sam Jr. out of the house, to set him on a more positive trajectory, but in the summer of 1962, when Sam was 16, and I was 14, she took another shot. She tried to get Sam Jr. into the Mount Hermon School for Boys in western Massachusetts. While not quite as famous as other boarding schools in its literal and figurative league—Andover, Choate, Deerfield, Hotchkiss, Lawrenceville, Phillips Exeter, St. Paul's—Mount Hermon, now known as Northfield Mount Hermon, was equally distinguished.

The school was founded in 1809 by a minister named Dwight Lyman Moody, who foresaw an academy serving the sons of the region's farmers and manual laborers. Mount Hermon had a more egalitarian bent than other eastern prep schools, emphasizing the worth of physical work and agrarian ideals, reflecting the utopian energy emanating from New England at the time of its founding. Over the years its mission had evolved, and instead of educating the children of yeoman farmers and factory hands, Mount Hermon drew mostly from the same privileged pool of boys as Exeter and Lawrenceville.

I'm unsure how Katherine got my brother an admissions interview; likely it was the same connection that had landed us an audience at St. John the Divine a few years earlier. Or perhaps the Prestons piqued Katherine's interest; Alec, my best friend, would start at Andover in the fall.

Whatever the source of my mother's interest, she convinced Sam Jr. to apply and scheduled an interview with the Mount Hermon admissions office. As had been the case with St. Johns, I went along for the ride. We drove up to the village of Gill, Massachusetts, near the larger town of Greenfield, and I sat with my mother in the outer office while Sam and the admissions dean talked. After a half hour the dean came out, his face set, but he brightened a little when he saw me. He invited me in for a chat. The same thing happened as it had at choir school: The school rejected Sam, but I was invited to apply.

My acceptance at Mount Hermon School presented a dilemma for Dr. Sam. While he spent freely in some areas—cars, vacations, and altruistic missions—he was exceedingly frugal in others. And to give the man some due, he might have made a lot more money had he not so selflessly served the people of Middletown. He did fine as a family practice doc in a small town but could have done much better as a specialist or general-practice physician working in a city or suburb. Paying tuition at Mount Hermon could not be taken lightly.

Moreover, if I went away to school, I would escape his dominating influence. Also, instead of being proud of me, my father competed with me. He regarded my admission into a prestigious boarding school as a threat. On the other hand, my success reflected well on the family, and he constantly sought the approval of the community's upper echelon. The Prestons were sending their son to Andover, and the Shorters needed to keep up.

Dr. Sam grudgingly decided to send me to Mount Hermon but not before torturing me during one more ride-along to make house calls. "You're taking bread out of the mouths of your sisters and brothers, big shot," he warned me. "You better make good. You better not screw up."

And so for the fall of my sophomore year in high school, I left my sisters and brothers to fend for themselves (I repressed this fact; I didn't think about it), said so long to my buddies, took a final run on the streets near the park, and headed north to Mount Hermon. From the moment I stepped on campus, I felt more at home than I ever had on Highland Avenue.

I enrolled as a 10th grader, my childhood and secret past behind me. It was a picture book New England prep school, set on a bluff above the Connecticut River, nestled in a valley of the Berkshires. Unlike St. John's, Mount Hermon was a happy place—no homesick little kids crying themselves to sleep. Given the full docket of studies, sports, and activities, the absence of the house of horrors on Highland Avenue, and the fact that my morning classes were held just a short stroll across the quad from my dorm, I gave up my morning runs. In both the utilitarian and emotional realms, they were no longer necessary.

Although Mount Hermon boasted a strong cross-country program, regularly winning conference championships, I dived into the traditional team sports of football and baseball instead. I was on the small side but not scrawny. Unlike many kids who turn to distance running because they failed at other sports, I was a decent natural athlete possessed of good hand-eye coordination. I pitched and played first base and was voted co-captain of the JV baseball team.

The academic work was demanding, but I found my way, earning good grades in both the arts and sciences. Keeping to its egalitarian roots, Mount Hermon required each boy to perform 10 hours of weekly labor on campus, chores ranging from landscaping to office work to housekeeping. I was assigned a job in the dining hall, scraping plates after meals. Most boys complained about these tasks and tried to shirk them, but I always enjoyed working with my hands—the absorption, the focus, the routine.

I might never have returned to running (perhaps not for decades, when somebody else certainly would have catalyzed the running boom, and I would have anonymously jumped on the bandwagon), had it not been for another unique Mount Hermon tradition: the Bemis-Forslund Pie Race.

This little-known, awkwardly named event is in fact the oldest continuously run footrace in the United States, predating the Boston Marathon by eight years. The course stretches 4.3 miles around campus and the surrounding town, and every Mount Hermon student who completes the run in less than 33 minutes is rewarded with his own apple pie.

The race came around at the end of my sophomore year. Other than the running I did connected with football, baseball, and PE, I hadn't trained. But when the starting gun cracked, I was suddenly back in the streets of Middletown, losing myself in my morning run, hitting out my solitary rhythm. Now I sailed around the Pie Race course, drunk on the deep green spring and the wild energy of being 15.

The miles flew by. Somebody told me I had finished in seventh place. I subsequently learned that the first five finishers were the top runners on our school's champion cross-country team, and the sixth-place runner was the captain of our Nordic ski team. My performance drew the notice of Sam Green and Warren Hall, the cross-country coaches, who wanted me on their squad. The following September, instead of turning out for football, I toed the line for my first cross-country workout.

Big things were expected from that year's team. The boys who'd taken the top five spots in the previous spring's Pie Race were back. Coach Green barked at us to run the course, which carried 2.3 miles through the woods around campus. I finished fifth. My Pie Race performance had not been a fluke. There was public payoff to my boyhood eccentricity. Flushed with success, I returned to my Middletown ritual. In addition to the afternoon workouts with the team, I trained on my own, running in my spare time around the hilly, leafy campus.

As the autumn progressed, I worked my way up to second position on the team. My success boosted my self-confidence and buoyed my standing at the school. The dean of students took a liking to me and invited me to work for him in his office; I no longer had to scrape French toast crusts off the syrup-sticky plates in the dining hall. My chief duty was to take attendance at the chapel services that were then mandatory at our private school. The chore took only a few minutes and got me out of attending the service. I used that time for my morning run.

On a Friday morning in November 1963, I went through this drill during chapel, making a quick check mark next to the names of my classmates, concluding by checking off my own name. Then I broke away for my run, which felt all the sweeter because my classmates were confined in the chapel. I listened to the solemn strains of a hymn as I moved into the leaf-strewn late-autumn woods.

I returned just as the service was wrapping up. I entered through the boiler room of the building, where the maintenance man kept his headquarters. I felt at ease among my classmates from Westchester County, the Main Line, and the Back Bay, but I felt a special bond with the school's townie day students. I liked hanging around the workers who made the school run, and I enjoyed my moments moving through the boiler room, where the air was redolent of diesel oil and the custodian's cheap cigars. But on that morning, two steps into the room, I sensed that something was off, something was wrong. The custodian sat stone-faced over his transistor radio. In Dallas that day, President Kennedy had been shot and killed.

The JFK assassination, of course, formed a watershed moment of my Baby Boom generation. Those of us of a certain age recall our exact whereabouts during those moments. Mine always seemed inextricably connected to running.

4

Yahoo the Start

Our cross-country team was led by Mr. Samuel Green, but the assistant coach, Warren Hall, had a bigger influence on me. Warren was a young teacher, in his early- to mid-20s, recently graduated from Wabash College in Indiana, where he had been a standout in cross-country and track. Warren paced us through workouts. He was easy to talk to and relate to, and of course, during training runs our goal was either to keep up with him or beat him. Warren told us that that was the wrong approach. On easy days go easy, he told us. Don't compete on an easy run. Save that for the hard days.

On those hard days, Warren had us do hill repeats, often several sessions a week. Those two basic ideas—on easy days go easy, on hard days go all out; and the efficacy of hill training—stayed with me all through my career. Warren Hall was my first running mentor; George Bowman, the senior captain of our team, was the second. George led more by deed than by word. From him I learned how to comport myself, how to bring my best to every workout or race, even when I wasn't feeling my best. I learned from him how to encourage and support my teammates; how to carry and conduct myself. He taught me never to give up on a race, to always work through to the finish.

George also communicated one specific tactic that proved invaluable: In cross-country you had to start fast; otherwise, you might get buried amid the slop and roil of the opening. Yahoo the start, stick with the lead pack, and wait for your moment. This lesson that I learned from George Bowman at Mount Hermon School was the same lesson I would employ years later at the Olympic Marathon in Munich.

The teaching and example of these two mentors laid the bedrock for my education in running. At the conference championships, held in those stunned, muted, surreal days following the JFK assassination, Mount Hermon took the team title. George won the individual championship, and I finished fifth overall.

The following year, my senior year at Mount Hermon, I succeeded George as captain of the cross-country and track teams. I had spent the summer training hard in Middletown, running the streets twice a day. I often ran bare-chested, and little did I suspect that Valerie Kilcoin, a neighbor and classmate through my early school years, would sometimes sneak to the window of her bedroom to watch me run past.

"I thought Frank was such a dreamboat," Valerie would laughingly tell a reporter decades later. "He was the kindly, wonderful doctor's son home from his high-class boarding school. He lived in a big, beautiful house, and he was such a beautiful runner. I thought Frank had the perfect life."

Of course, Valerie had no idea about the true nature of the "kindly, wonderful doctor" who provided his family the opposite of a perfect life. Indeed, if anyone in our family lived according to his desires, it was our father, for whom public good and private evil existed in equipoise, one side of his nature feeding the other in dark symbiosis. He relied on healing to give spice to his hurting and expiated his crimes by delivering babies and saving children from polio.

But now I had my refuge, Mount Hermon, and now I had an escape route that also formed a path to retribution: running. I excelled during the cross-country season in the fall of my senior year, setting course records everywhere we competed, from Deerfield to Choate to Exeter. During the spring track season, I was conference champion in the 2-mile and finished second in the 1-mile. Had I been a public school kid, I might have been recruited by an NCAA track power such as Villanova, but college coaches didn't pay much attention to preppies. When it came to selecting a college, I was on my own.

While there were no athletic scholarship offers, I had a relatively strong hand to play—high class ranking, good SAT scores and teacher recommendations, and my running success. I applied to Yale and Williams, with Hobart as my safety school. Yale was my first choice, due both to its academic stature and the fact that it had a strong track program, led by longtime head coach Bob Giegengack, who had amassed a long string of Ivy League titles and had served as head coach of the 1964 US Olympic track-and-field team.

My choice of colleges, this transition point in my life, put my father in another difficult position, one he dealt with by denial. One of Dr. Sam's subtle but potent weapons was his total lack of interest in any pursuit important to his children. I don't recall his attending a single parent-teacher conference. For all my success as an athlete, he never watched me run, never asked me about my sport. The same held true for all my siblings. In his twisted way, he regarded us as competitors—for what prize only he could imagine. If he ignored our accomplishments, he wouldn't feel threatened by them.

The college acceptance letters arrived during spring break of my senior year. I was admitted to all three schools; my heart was set on Yale.

As was the case with Mount Hermon, Yale was expensive. Dr. Sam made too much money for us to qualify for need-based assistance, and Ivy League schools didn't award athletic scholarships. On the other hand, the distinction of having his son go to Yale was too attractive to pass up. I could go to Yale, but it would be a financial stretch, a fact he never let me forget for my first few years at the university. "You're taking bread out of your sisters' and brothers' mouths," he would tell me.

+ + +

My mother took me to New Haven for the start of my freshman year in September 1965. America was starting to ferment, change, blossom, and metastasize. I felt it mostly unconsciously; it was there in the songs on my transistor radio. I was pretty straight, your basic preppy with a little bit of a populist bent. Politically, I was a Kennedy Democrat; a narrow-tie and blazer and desert boot–type kid, my genes steeped in generations of WASP reticence and stoicism.

My family suffered enormously due to this reluctance to raise a fuss. Why hadn't a concerned uncle or aunt followed up on his or her suspicion that, despite appearances, something wasn't quite right with Dr. Sam and the house on Highland Avenue? Why weren't there ever any extended-family holiday gatherings at a house that seemed designed for them? How come the doc's kids had such trouble looking you in the eye? Why didn't someone break through the veneer of gentility and modesty to rescue us? No family savior stepped forward. My father maintained his act, and the rest of the family either played along or looked the other way.

The extended family, however, was rock-solid in its respect for education, and I had hit the jackpot, matriculating at Yale. To mark the occasion, my grandmother, Ida, my mother's mother, a Phi Beta Kappa member herself, traveled with us to New Haven. Despite my outward calm, I felt anxious. Of the eleven boys in my dorm suite, six had either been valedictorians or salutatorians of their high school senior class. I was just a skinny, secretly battered kid from a small town in upstate New York. Yale was going to be a challenge, but I was willing to find out if I could make it.

After I got settled into my dorm, I went out for a run with Steve Bittner, who would also be one of my teammates on the freshman cross-country team. As soon as I took my first step, I calmed down. I realized that running—and the friendship of my fellow runners—would form my refuge for the next four years. I liked all the guys, and 50 years later they are still my friends. Every August, a bunch of us get together to run the Hood to Coast Relay in Oregon.

Yale. You studied from morning through the night. The workload was crushing for a premed major. You would think in my determination not to become like Dr. Sam, I would have stampeded away from medicine. But instead, more unconsciously than otherwise, I chose to compete with my father. I was good at the sciences and despite my father's example—despite looking at that caduceus tattoo every time that man raised his hand to me, despite the fleck of brain matter he'd sadistically shown me on that spectral Thanksgiving night, and despite the horror of those schizophrenic house calls—I respected the medical profession and believed that healing formed a high calling. Moreover, in Dr. Preston, the father of my best friend in Middletown, I had had a positive role model, a physician who served with no secret agenda or ulterior motive.

So I turned on my desk lamp and started to grind. Calculus, physics, organic chemistry: The sciences were my bread and butter, but I also felt drawn to the humanities and social sciences. Learning in general appealed to me, and I was surrounded by a wealth of great teachers. One of them was my coach, Bob Giegengack. He was a wonderful man, a native of Brooklyn with a speech impediment that made him sound like a Flatbush Elmer Fudd. But it was a mistake to underestimate him. A Phi Beta Kappa graduate in classics at Holy Cross University, Gieg had a deep understanding of the middle distances and brought a scientific approach to training. He had come to Yale in 1946, and his teams had won four IC4A championships and 17 Heptagonal meet titles, the true measure of success at Yale. The Heps encompassed all the Ivy League schools, plus Army and Navy.

Gieg was a proponent of laying a firm foundation in training, based on the same principles that my coaches at Mount Hermon had instilled. Then he let each athlete decide for himself how hard he was going to work and how he might adapt the training once he'd mastered the fundamentals. Gieg also understood that his mission wasn't to produce champion runners; it was to produce good Yale men. The championships and trophies came as a by-product of following the high-achieving Yale way. A young runner just sort of imbibed excellence, and part of that excellence resulted from not over-emphasizing results. Academics and general comportment—being a student and a gentleman—always came first.

That suited me. I grasped the dynamic and got into the rhythm. Back in Middletown, I employed running as an escape from my father's abuse, and now I ran to blow off the stress of intense studying. The hour and a half a day I spent training never felt like work; instead, it was always a relief and a privilege.

I was the top runner on our freshman cross-country team but didn't stand out in the larger arena. In fact, I never even won a meet title until my senior year. Before that I had had two runner-up finishes, in both races placing a distant second to Doug Hardin of Harvard, Yale's archrival. On the regional or national NCAA radar, I raised not a blip.

Instead of pouring everything I had into the sport, defining myself by how well or poorly I'd performed in my last race, I drilled down on the books and worked on becoming a well-rounded Yale man—in Ivy League parlance, a "protean man." I made a lot of good friends, took classes from distinguished scholars such as the anthropologist Margaret Mead, the novelist and classicist Erich Segal, and the art historian Vincent Scully. I joined a singing group on campus, and during spring break junior year, instead of traveling down to Florida with the track team, I went on a southern tour with my choral group. By chance, the track team bus passed us as we traveled south out of New Haven; I remember waving to my teammates in the other bus.

Still, through it all, beneath it all, I realized that somehow, in some way, running would form my true calling. I enjoyed learning in all its aspects, but I knew that I could only become an expert— could only hope to distinguish myself—in one area: running. Other people appeared to reach the same conclusion. Selection to a secret society, for instance, was a high ambition for many Yale undergrads. The most famous society was Skull and Bones, whose influential members include the Bush father and his eldest son.

There were about a half-dozen others, admitting a relative handful of seniors each year. Selection came during "tap night"; you sat at your desk in your dorm room and waited for a knock on your door. Unless you earned good grades and stood out in at least one extracurricular area, you waited in vain. Indeed, some students engaged in "club grubbing," padding their résumés to look better to the clubs, much in the way that some high school kids pad their résumés to look good to college admissions officers.

I was the opposite of a club grubber. Besides dabbling as a vocalist, my only outside activity was running, and I didn't think that was enough to make the grade. But to my surprise, on tap night, I felt a tap on my shoulder. I'd been chosen to join the Berzilius Society, whose members formed a cross-section of Yale undergraduates, encompassing science, drama, and humanities students, as well as members of the then-underground gay community. I was tapped, the members explained to me, largely due to my running.

Still, my performances didn't indicate that I had a future in the sport beyond college. In the late 1960s, only the very best collegiate runners could attain much of a career beyond school. Track and field was strictly an amateur proposition, and road racing as we know it today did not yet exist. You couldn't earn a living as a competitive runner, and few outlets enabled you to continue running as an amateur. Moreover, I was a runner at Yale. In the national arena, no one took an Ivy League athlete seriously.

At the end of my sophomore year, however, the picture started to change. Ironically, the catalyst emerged out of the very place I thought I'd escaped: my family.

5

Western Skies

In the summer of 1967, as abruptly as he'd decided to leave West Virginia and return to Middletown 20 years earlier—and as suddenly as he would pull up the family and stuff us into the station wagon for one of our "vacations," which would start in a spirit of adventure but quickly devolve into theater for our father's terrifying fits of road rage—Dr. Sam decided to pull up stakes and move to Taos, New Mexico. Ostensibly, he was going west to continue saving the world, this time as the head of a Presbyterian mission hospital serving the Latino community of northern New Mexico.

That might have been the main motivation, but other pressures also helped drive him out of town. I had long suspected my father of philandering. He hit on my sisters' teenage friends, and some of the supposedly routine "house calls" to female patients would mysteriously stretch for an hour or more. Also, while an impeccable clinician, Dr. Sam was less sterling in the business aspects of his practice. His billing system was haphazard, and he took a cavalier attitude toward paying taxes. In fact, we would later learn that he hadn't paid his IRS bill for several years. Perhaps the walls were closing in on Dr. Sam in Middletown, so the doc decamped for the wide open spaces of the West.

The move produced a number of consequences for me, all positive. My father took a pay cut when he arrived in Taos, where he worked at a clinic operated as a mission by the Presbyterian Church. His income was reduced enough that I qualified for financial aid from Yale, which dispensed aid purely on a need basis. For my final year at the university, I received what amounted to a full scholarship. Since I no longer had to rely on my father for financial support, he couldn't hold his grudging largesse over my head. No more guilt trips; no more harping that I was stealing the bread out of my siblings' mouths; and no more worring about Dr. Sam's chronically late tuition payments. I found this development liberating.

The second and more far-reaching consequence was that I discovered the Mountain West. Given the darkness enveloping my family, you might think that I never would've wanted to go home; that I would've seized on any pretext for staying on campus, visiting friends, or traveling during breaks from college. But that wasn't the case. As much as I hated the house on Highland Avenue, I loved the people of Middletown (I still love the town today, returning each June to run the Middletown 10-K road race), and once my family moved to New Mexico, I was anxious to maintain connection with my siblings, keeping a big brother's eye on them.

The summer after my sophomore year, I found a job in New Mexico lifeguarding and cleaning bathrooms at Ghost Ranch, a Presbyterian retreat; and after my junior year, I worked for the Taos-area natural gas company, El Paso Natural Gas, digging ditches. I lived part of the time at home, but mostly at a dorm at the ranch. These were great what-the-hell jobs under the high-desert sunshine, in the crystal mountain air. I tore around with a bunch of other college boys working at the ranch. My janitorial supervisor at Ghost Ranch, a Latino woman named Josie, took a liking to us. She would sneak us extra food and occasionally buy us a six-pack of beer. One day she asked us if we wanted to meet this artist lady whose house she cleaned on the side. The artist's name was Georgia O'Keefe.

Of course I jumped at the opportunity to meet the world-famous painter who was practically synonymous with New Mexico. Josie came by in a pickup truck, and we piled onto the truck bed and rattled down the desert roads to Ms. O'Keefe's adobe house. A spare, severe woman with the luminous eyes portrayed in the iconic photographs of her husband, Alfred Stieglitz, Ms. O'Keefe met us on the porch. The other boys were starstruck. I was in awe, too, but at the same time I felt curious. I wanted to find out about her. In turn, she asked about me. I said that I went to Yale and had taken an art history class from Vincent Scully, in which I'd studied her work. I told her that, despite being color-blind, I loved how she rendered the New Mexico light. I explained that instead of writing about a painting for my grade, I had arranged with Mr. Scully to do a special project on pueblo architecture. Ms. O'Keefe seemed to approve of this.

After a few minutes we left. Later, I didn't brag about meeting a great artist. What had impressed me was that Georgia O'Keefe had taken the time to meet some boys brought to her by the woman who cleaned her house.

The true gift of New Mexico, however, was the opportunity to train at altitude. Most afternoons after I got off work, I would go for a run at 7,000-foot elevation around town or at 9,000-foot elevation at Taos Ski Valley. I wasn't deliberately trying to altitude-train, to boost my red blood count and oxygen-delivery capacity, but those first runs at altitude planted the idea in my brain and started to put steel in my body.

There wasn't much to show for it in terms of performance when I returned to school in the fall. Again, I finished a distant second to my Harvard rival Doug Hardin at the Heptagonal cross-country championships, and again, I buried myself in my premed studies, emerging for an hour a day to clear my head and heart with a run. I developed into the top distance runner at Yale and one of the better runners in the Ivies, but I hardly qualified as national-class material, let alone demonstrated Olympic-level potential. Instead, I appeared to be on a solid track to graduate and enter medical school and fall in step with the tide of American life.

By this time the tide had turned turbulent. The 1960s had descended with full force on American campuses, hitting Yale particularly hard. I was sympathetic to the counterculture—I liked the Beatles and was against the Vietnam War, and I grew a mustache and longish hair—but I viewed developments with a certain coolness, from a characteristic remove. I was no conservative—I wanted to help change things and sensed the temper of the times— but at heart I was more of a traditionalist.

Given the punishment I endured from my father, I well might have hated the establishment and seized the opportunity that history provided to vent my hurt and anger in marches and protests, but I didn't feel that way. When considering the older generation, I didn't think of the evil Dr. Sam; I thought instead of Dr. and Mrs. Preston, of Mr. Parmalee at the Y, of the kind Mexican woman who had introduced me to Georgia O'Keefe, and of my coach, Bob Giegengack. Rather than not trusting anyone over 30, I craved the affection and approval of my elders.

Besides, I already had a vent for my pain—I had running. I also had Yale. I was aware of the richness surrounding me at the school. Rather than rebel, I resolved to learn all I could in order to effect meaningful long-term change. My thinking was in step with my racing style: Go out with the leaders and wait for the time to make my definitive move. I took a dim view of the campus sit-ins and shutdowns. They interfered with my education. More disturbing, they interrupted my training, and training was sacred.

I capped my junior track season by qualifying for the 5000 at the NCAA championships, which were held that year at UC Berkeley. Gieg sent all Yale qualifiers to NCAA meets, even if they had no chance of scoring points, and I clearly fell into that category. I ran an okay but not great 13:55, finishing far out of contention— behind Kerry Pearce and Gerry Lindgren.

And then came the sea change, which began the summer after my junior year. It started with the family I was so desperate to escape. At the close of the academic year in New Haven, I again traveled to New Mexico to be close to my siblings in case they needed me and also to earn some money; my scholarship stipulated that I had to work and provide some of my own funding. Ken Levan, my sister Susan's boyfriend and future husband, found me a job digging ditches for the natural gas company in the town of Aztec, near Farmington. Ken was a great guy, and I bunked happily in a spare bedroom at his parents' house. For me, a simple family home emanating basic affection and respect seemed a wonder. To a degree, such a place still seems a miracle today. When I travel to speaking engagements around the country, I always request to stay in a private home rather than in a hotel.

I stayed with Ken's parents, but I saw my sisters and brothers often. My father was around the house even less in New Mexico than he'd been in Middletown, but his general MO remained the same. In fact, like most addictive behaviors, his sociopathic ways worsened. My brother Michael was born—my mother's near-continuous skein of pregnancies continued—and he quite obviously was a Down syndrome child. I had taken a child psychology class at Yale, and even I recognized the condition. But my father, a seasoned family physician who had delivered hundreds of babies, refused to accept the diagnosis or admit to any kind of problem. Indeed, as soon as Michael got old enough, Dr. Sam started wailing on the boy: He was so sick that he pounded a Down syndrome kid. (That finally got to be too much for my mother, and she divorced him in 1975 . . . but that is getting ahead of my story.)

One day my sister Amie, who was around 11 at the time, suffered a serious wig-out. Episodes of violent acting out were understandably common around the Shorter household, but this time, Amie raged and wept and was generally inconsolable. I tried to reason with her, but I don't think my voice even got through to her. Finally, my mother summoned my father from his clinic 20 miles away—this had never happened before. Dr. Sam came home, and my sister finally quieted. A phone call came for my father from the local hospital. He hung up the phone and turned to poor Amie with that all too familiar blood in his eye. "Because I had to rush home and take care of you, one of my patients died," he told the hysterical girl, as if she needed another reason to feel miserable.

Luckily for me, I could readily escape our western house of horrors. I worked all day on the roads swinging a pick in the pure high-desert sunlight, and then after work I would run the high-altitude dirt roads for hours. Then I would return home to Ken's house—perhaps have a few beers and watch some TV—and then go into a deep blackout sleep before climbing back on the wheel the next morning. I felt myself getting stronger. Some afternoons, running the trails, I felt as swift and weightless as the hawks wheeling in the blue sky overhead. It seemed I was getting faster by the minute. As the summer deepened, a certainty grew that I was approaching a breakthrough. I didn't know it yet, but running was going to deliver me someplace special.

I returned to Yale for my senior year. Most of my killer premed courses were in the can, but I still had to keep up my GPA for med school admissions—not many slots were open in those days, and I had a big senior research project to finish and file. But now I ran more confidently, with a sense of mission. I won all but one Ivy League cross-country meet, much in the way that I'd excelled against the Exeters and Andovers back during my senior year of prep school. My second-place finish at the Heptagonal cross-country championships qualified me for the NCAA Championship Meet, held that year at Van Cortlandt Park in the Bronx. Unlike my experience at the track NCAAs in Berkeley the previous spring, I was in the hunt at this race. I took myself more seriously, even if few others gave an Ivy League athlete much of a shot.

The gun cracked, and as I'd learned from George Bowman back at Mount Hermon, I yahooed the start, spurting away from the line so that I wouldn't get swallowed by the pack. It was a 10-K course, the longer the better by my lights; those hard sun-splashed summer miles at Rocky Mountain altitude had strengthened me externally and internally. At the 5-mile mark I was in sixth place, within striking distance of the lead or at least with the chance to score some solid points for the Bulldogs. Over the last mile the pack caught up with me. I had not yet attained my full strength, or, more accurately, I did not yet fully believe in my own strength. I hung on to finish 19th, within the top 20, which officially made me an All-American, and NCAA All-Americans were the one thing in short supply at Yale University.

Thus encouraged, I sailed into winter and the indoor track season (training and racing mostly on the funky track of Cox Cage, the Yale field house), when I broke through to the next level. My indoor times were competitive with the best collegiate runners in the country, and in February 1969, on the track at the Joe Louis Arena in Detroit, I finished a close second in the NCAA championships in the 2-mile. Still, my proudest moment of that breakout indoor season occurred in the Heptagonal championship meet held at the newly dedicated Jadwin Gym at Princeton. The top runner for our archrival Harvard was a 4:01 miler named Royce Shaw.

I was entered in the race with my teammate Steve Bittner. On the last lap, Steve and I both passed Shaw, finishing first and second in a dead heat, setting a new Yale record for the mile, 4:06.7. We had beaten the star Harvard man at his specialty. And the mile wasn't really my métier. I was a longer-distance guy.

Now it was time for the 2-mile, which was more in my wheelhouse. Harvard had another stud in this event, a guy named Doug Hardin, who bore an uncanny resemblance to Woody Allen (Doug also happened to be a virtuoso cellist and served as class marshal at the Harvard commencement ceremony). I went out with Hardin. He and I pulled away from the pack, and over the final mile we were alone in front, hammering stride-for-stride. The Crimson crowd was going nuts; they were sure their man would prevail, but for the last eight laps I knew that I had this one nailed. I waited, waited . . . and finally at the bell lap, with 200 yards to go, I cut loose, blowing past Hardin and winning by a 20-yard margin.

So on that winter day I had beaten both Harvard stars at their specialties and in a meet where I was doubling. That gave me confidence. Those two races told me I was developing the ability to close faster than my competitors; I could launch my finishing surge earlier and maintain it longer. Put simply, I had located a higher gear; I had learned that I had the ability to run fast when I was tired, the prime trait of a top-shelf distance runner.

Those performances qualified me for the NCAA Indoor Championships; my third consecutive national championship appearance in three different running disciplines. And unlike the outdoor and cross-country nationals, I was a contender at the indoors. My opponents suddenly regarded me in a different light. Competing in the 2-mile, I finished a close second behind Ole Ollessen, a highly regarded runner from the University of Southern California, a traditional NCAA track power.

The winter wound down, and the spring semester opened. I filed my senior research project ahead of schedule—I have always been punctual about deadlines and hate to have overdue projects hanging over my head—and now, for the first time since entering Yale, I had the opportunity to focus solely on running, to see if I could get this sport right. I sat down with Coach Giegengack, who had been directing my training with an increasingly light hand. By the time we were seniors, he expected his athletes to be essentially coaching themselves. Gieg encouraged me to keep following my instincts; he told me that I could take running as far as I wanted. Gieg was the quintessential college coach, but he had also served as head coach of the 1964 US Olympic track-and-field team in Tokyo, where he had guided Billy Mills to an unlikely gold in the 10,000 meters. My coach looked me in the eye. I understood his meaning.

I started training twice a day several days a week. I had now figured out that my particular talent lay in the long distances, the 5000- and 10,000-meter (in those premetric-system days, American runners competed in the 3-mile and 6-mile) events on the track. Road races at these distances, now staples in towns and cities around the world, did not yet exist. The marathon, meanwhile, was a forbidding and exotic enterprise that occurred only rarely: The Boston Marathon was run each April, and the Fukuoka Marathon in Japan every December. The Olympic Marathon came around only once every four years. I thought I might do well in the marathon, but for right now my future lay on the track. I decided that the key to success in the 5 and 10 was building speed in the shorter distances.

The conventional thinking in distance training placed greater emphasis on endurance, building a base by piling up miles run at an aerobic pace. I thought that a deep base of endurance was essential to keep you in the race, but speed—4:06-mile speed, 56-second 400 speed—was necessary to win. So you had to work on both ends: Run the hard sessions—that is, the intervals measuring 1200 meters or less—very hard, and the long runs at a pace at which you recovered from the hard intervals. I started experimenting, trying to find a formula simple enough to be applied consistently that incorporated and synthesized all I had learned in Middletown, Mount Hermon, New Haven, and Taos: Amass a high-volume, high-quality weekly mileage; log two hard track workouts during the week; and on the weekend knock out a long run at an aerobic pace adjusted to the perceived effort of the shorter work. Each of these building blocks was important, but the quality of my speedwork—those gut-busting twice-weekly interval sessions—was what I instinctively knew would set me apart. I just seemed to be good at this type of training, and I loved it. My goal was to finish each speed workout by running the fastest interval of the day. At the end of the workout, had someone held a gun to my head and ordered me to run one more interval, my answer would have been, "Go ahead and shoot."

So through the first cold days of 1969, as Richard Nixon brooded over the map of Cambodia and in the Sangre de Cristo Mountains of New Mexico my father ministered to the poor Latinos and Pueblo Indians by day and afflicted his children at night,

I imposed an internal and external order by knocking out hard, solitary 7-mile morning runs on the slushy lanes of campus and two afternoons a week embraced the crucible of intervals—10 × 400, 6 × a mile—on the boards of Cox Cage, the Yale field house, or later, as the spring thaw took hold, on the outdoor track on campus.

During spring break that year there was no more larking with the choral group. I traveled with the track team down to the Florida Relays, a key early season meet that would signal the prospects for the major meets later in the spring. There we prevailed over the traditional eastern powers in the distance-medley relay. I ran a 4.07-mile leg to key Yale's victory. In the open 2-mile individual race, I toed the line beside Jack Bacheler, a storklike, 6'7" runner from Miami University of Ohio, who would later become a close friend and ally along with another tall guy, John Parker of the University of Florida, who would also become my comrade.

My experience at the Florida Relays, meeting Jack and John, influenced my decision to move to Gainesville the following spring. I admired Jack's combination of fierceness and consideration, and John projected a similar vibe. You could be close friends one minute and the next, on the track, try to beat each other's brains out. The intensity of competition deepened the quality of our friendship and vice versa. A little later I would become friends with Steve Prefontaine, who personified this ethic.

Spring break ended, and we traveled back north. At the big IC4A meet at Rutgers, I finished second in the 5000 and again qualified for the outdoor NCAA championships, which were held that year at the University of Tennessee in Knoxville. It was the season of roil and discord across America. During those years, National Guard troops opened fire on the kids on the hill at Kent

State and John and Yoko spooned naked together on the cover of *Rolling Stone* magazine. ROTC buildings were torched, and classes were cancelled as students marched solemnly in antiwar candle-light marches.

I did not join all that. Not that I wasn't stirred by developments; not that I failed to feel the pulse of my time. I just felt that my role was to wait and listen and learn, to build my strength and knowledge so I could pick my battles instead of reacting to events. Make my shot count instead of firing wildly. Also, I deeply resented any interruption of my training. I was just getting into the rhythm, just starting to sing in key. I sensed my destiny and would not be derailed.

Classes were over. Where should I go? My parents and sister Barbara were visiting Middletown, and I decided to spend a few days with them before returning to New Haven for commencement ceremonies. Middletown was finally changing, the lawn mower factory closing as the world shifted to power mowers; the mills shuttering and the jobs moving south. Downtown hollowed out as shopping malls sprouted on the highway at the edge of town. Commuting executives from New York City moved into the graceful Dutch colonials, and the city's cops and firefighters flocked to the ranch-style subdivisions rising near the malls.

My old town was disappearing, but I continued to run on Highland Avenue past the Y, through the park near where the Prestons still lived. One day I gave Barbara a stopwatch, and we drove down to the cinder track at Middletown High School. I took off my shirt, and with Barbara timing me, I slammed around the slow cinder track 24 times, covering 6 miles in 30 minutes flat. My sister watched, amazed at first at how fast I was moving, but then, as the laps and miles accrued, she grew bored, waving to friends in the parking lot. My plan was working. I was ready to graduate.

The NCAA Championship Meet in Knoxville took place on a day as hot and humid as you might expect in Tennessee in June. The 6-mile was first on my docket. I went out hard, hung with the lead pack until midrace, and then, drawing on all those intervals, that 4:06-mile speed, threw down a surge that opened a 100-meter lead. No one was able to close that gap, and I won in 29:00.2, 23 seconds ahead of Rick Riley of Washington State, the second-place finisher. I was an NCAA champion. Coaches, athletes, and fans from outside the Northeast wondered, who is this Yalie?

The next day, in the 3-mile finals, I finished second in 13:43.4, a whisker behind a runner from Southern Cal named Ole Ollesson, who ran 13:42.0. My victory the day before hadn't been a fluke. Moreover, that meet demonstrated my ability to quickly recover; no other runner attempted the punishing 6-mile/3-mile double.

Things were starting to move faster now. My experiments were bearing fruit. I was working very hard, but it didn't feel like work. My Knoxville performances qualified me for the following week's national AAU championships, which included post-collegiate runners and Olympic hopefuls, although there were no professionals in those days. The meet was held at the University of Miami. Even though I'd graduated and was no longer officially running for Yale, Bob Giegengack graciously paid for my trip to Florida.

I had qualified in both the 6 and the 3 but decided only to race the 6, my strongest distance. My chief competition consisted of Jack Bacheler, the defending national champion in the event, a runner named Juan Martinez, and Kenny Moore, a University of Oregon graduate and 1968 Olympian in the marathon who now competed for the US Army track team. This race was the biggest challenge thus far in my career; I was a boy running against men, but I hung in. Jack won, successfully defending his title. Martinez finished second, and Kenny and I duked it out for the valuable third-place spot; the top finishers would make the national team that would travel to Europe that summer. Kenny out-leaned me at the wire, and afterward he seemed more relieved than celebratory.

"If I had finished fourth, the army would have taken me off the track team and sent me for advanced infantry training," Kenny explained. "And after that you go straight to Nam."

I was disappointed about not going to Europe but philosophical: I was really just getting started as a serious distance runner. Then a bolt of good news struck: Jack Bacheler decided to finish his graduate work in entomology that summer and turned down his spot on the team. I was next up due to my strong finish, and I eagerly packed my bags for Europe.

The central event of the tour would be a dual meet between the United States and a team composed of Europe's best track-and-field athletes. The United States had long dominated global track and field, but our strength lay in the sprints and jumps and throws. American Olympic distance-running medalists such as Billy Mills and Bob Schul were outliers; European runners and coaches composed the gold standard. I had a lot to learn about my craft, and I couldn't wait to get started.

Another first-timer on the national team that summer was a talented young middle-distance runner from Coos Bay, a lumber-mill town on the coast of southern Oregon. His name was Steve Prefontaine, and he had just graduated from Marshfield High School. He was headed to the University of Oregon to run for Bill Bowerman and his assistant coach, Bill Dellinger. Pre—that was his nickname; everybody called him Pre—had finished second in the 5000 to earn his spot on the national team in Europe. It had been an electric, swashbuckling, risk-taking, front-running performance. With a shock of blonde hair and glinting blue eyes, Pre, even at age 18, possessed a presence that communicated passion and excitement. He was one of those "mad ones" that Jack Kerouac chased after and wrote about. Pre and I were opposites in just about every regard— geographic location, age, class, and education. I was a quintessential East Coast Yalie (at least by appearance), and he was the model of a logging-town westerner. But we occupied the same seldom-visited athletic neighborhood, long-distance running, so we were thrown together.

We quickly learned that we shared a gift: a combination of genetic, behavioral, and environmental characteristics that enabled us to run fast when we were tired and in pain. In the chicken-egg nature of our enterprise, this meant that in training we were willing to spend a great deal of time feeling hurt and exhausted. Pre's interval training and mine were very similar. The idea was to run your repeats very hard and fast, and key the pace of your other training to the intensity of your intervals. A typical interval session might consist of 4×1200 or 6×800.

Early in that European tour, the first week out, Pre and I met for a workout in Augsburg, Germany. It was a ladder session: mile, 1600, 1200, 800, 800, 400, 400, during which you run faster with each successive repeat. This is the hardest work a runner has to endure, and very quickly, within the first few reps, you can discern the nature and character of your training partner. Some guys never take the lead, forcing you to beat into the wind and maintain the draining pace. This is okay if the other runner is weaker, but sometimes guys are capable of the task but shrink from it—a different kind of weakness. Other runners will discuss the work in detail, meeting the responsibility of sharing pacesetting. These guys, while honorable, aren't much fun. The workouts proceed in a clenched, grim, scripted fashion. You log the work, but there isn't much juice or passion.

Then there is the rare third kind of runner, one who shares your ability but more importantly shares your sense of honor, your sense of what it means to be a runner. You are fellow members in a guild of pain and sacrifice, which, in those distant amateur days, was mostly its own reward. With this caliber of training partner, you don't need a script or a plan or orders from a coach. You just look into one another's eyes, see that understanding of the code, and then you go about your work, trading off on the lead, hitting a rhythm that makes the pain bearable, productive, and at certain points, fiercely pleasurable. More than the wins, more than the fast times, this brotherhood—this trust—forms the heart of the sport.

From the moment we toed the line for that first repeat on a Tuesday afternoon in July 1969, Pre and I shared this unspoken bond. We shared the burden every moment of that workout. We knocked out some searing times: the 1600 in 4:12, the 1200 in 3:09, two 800s in 2:04 and 2:00 respectively, two 400s in 56 and 57 seconds respectively. By the end of it we both realized that we were on to something with our training—and that we had found a kind of brother in one another. We drew energy from each other. We weren't trying to impress. Instead, we genuinely wanted the other guy to prosper. You cheer on your teammates—you even encourage your opponents—because you understand and admire the effort they're putting in. That's what I miss now—not the obvious pleasure of winning a race or achieving a personal record (PR), but of going to the track for a hard interval workout and experiencing that brotherhood in action.

Pre and I continued working out together during that summer, all through the UK and finishing up in Poland. I was coaching myself, and Pre was getting his workouts from Dellinger, but our training philosophies were remarkably similar. We both realized that what we were doing was working. This sort of chemistry doesn't happen often. I was glad I had found this kid from the wild coast of Oregon. We didn't hang out much, but on the track we both thought the same way. Pre was mature beyond his years. All the stuff about Steve Prefontaine being an uncoachable wild man was just BS.

6

Road Runner Once, Road Runner Twice

The summer came to an end, and now it was time to go back to the States, back to reality. I now knew that my running was leading me somewhere. Over the last year I had progressed from a good but not great Ivy League athlete to an NCAA champion and one of the top-ranked 10,000-meter runners in the nation. From my perspective, the intellectual adventure in self-coaching was almost as gratifying as the results on the track. I knew that I was just getting started, and I was hungry—ravenous—to see how far it would take me. But where was I going to go, how was I going to support myself, in what manner would I make good on the investment made in my Yale education? In 1970 there were no running-shoe companies to sponsor training groups or offer endorsement contracts. You couldn't win money at road races because professional road races didn't exist. You faced a starving-artist existence, scratching along in grad school or the army if you got drafted. I chose a somewhat different path, enrolling in the University of New Mexico (UNM) medical school in Albuquerque.

Medical school had always been my goal, and I couldn't let one hot year on the track divert me from the path. (Also, the military draft was hanging over my head, something every young American man was preoccupied with at the time. Although I did not march or demonstrate, I was in line politically with most of my peers and opposed the Vietnam War. The fact that med school extended my student deferment formed a bonus.) With youthful hubris, I thought I could balance the crushing workload of med school with the equally demanding labor required of an elite distance runner.

I had applied to three medical schools—Yale, the University of California–San Francisco (UCSF), and UNM. Only UNM accepted me, which worked out for the best because I qualified for in-state tuition since my parents had moved to Taos. Also, Albuquerque was an ideal place to train, with sunny weather, mountain trails, and the track at the university. I was philosophical about the rejections from Yale and UCSF. In terms of academics, I was eager and inquisitive but what really inflamed my imagination was running. I wanted to become a doctor because I thought I should become a doctor—because I wanted to simultaneously follow my father and separate from him. Had I not discovered running, I probably would have stayed the course, soldiering through med school, choosing a suitable specialty, and serving as a competent, solid clinician. But I had discovered running, or running had found me, and instead my destiny followed an alternate course.

I started classes in September, linked up with some training partners from the university, and tried to live a double life; it didn't work. I dropped out of school after a month. The med school curriculum was demanding, but I also found it to be inefficient. The goal seemed to be to pile on the hours rather than master the material, leaving no time for anything else. I was aching to train; I had a window of time to blossom as a competitive runner, and I had to take advantage of it. I went to the med school dean, told her my story, and asked her if I could work out some accommodation that would allow me to go to school while preparing for the Olympic trials. I came to the meeting prepared; I even cited a study showing that sleep deprivation, common among med school students, actually hurt retention.

She thought it over and said sorry, they couldn't make any adjustments to my schedule. I could accept that. When I asked her to explain why, however, she really didn't have an answer.

"Because that's the way I did it," she said.

That sort of rigid thinking, that sort of denial, had always bothered me, maybe because denial had always been the central but unacknowledged fact of my own life.

I withdrew from medical school and threw my lot in with my sport. A few days later the dean came back to me, offering to work something out, but it was too late. I was already gone, already intent on pursuing my destiny as a runner.

I didn't have a plan for how I was going to live. I figured there were a lot of things I could do as long as running remained the focus. I wasn't going to let my window of opportunity close. I went back to my parents' house in Taos. It was hard to be around my father, even for the short chunks of time he was home, but I wanted to be near my siblings. I relished running in the high desert and mountains and had fallen in love with the West. When I wasn't running, I made myself useful by laying a new tile floor and helping to build an addition on to the back of the house. At the NCAA meet the previous June I had met a runner from the University of Texas at El Paso, who told me the city was cheap to live in and had good places to train. I rode the Greyhound down to El Paso, felt the heat, and saw the power relays jutting over the concrete banks of the Rio Grande; I quickly hopped on a bus back to New Mexico.

I went back to running, back to working around the house, and back to unconsciously plotting my father's moves and moving out of his way to keep my sisters and brothers out of the line of fire. I felt grateful that my stay here was only temporary, that soon I'd be leaving to continue my escape, that I'd found a path out through Yale, through my sport, and through the kindness, counsel, and example of mentors and friends. But in that first season out of college, behind the enthusiasm and optimism I experienced while running under the high blue sky and in the crystalline light that Georgia O'Keefe rendered so unforgettably, I also returned to feeling that black, barely perceptible tug of guilt for not being able to save the rest of my family.

Because Dr. Sam still raged. Rending episodes like the one with my sister Amie ensued. That was an episode I remember. There were many others I have blotted out. I now regarded my father with something approaching clinical dispassion—my education and my years away had lent me some critical distance. My father was a rare human being, a man who didn't want his children to thrive, whose hopes for his offspring did not exceed his twisted hopes for himself. He tried to undermine every interest and ambition his children embraced. I think he was secretly pleased that I had dropped out of medical school, but my achievements and ambitions as an athlete threatened him. He had never seen one of my races or track meets. He never asked about my running or showed any curiosity or support. Not until the infamous episode that started out on the highway.

The roads and trails in northern New Mexico were ideal for training, but I was the only person out running in those days. The Santa Fe–Taos nexus had long formed a colony for artists and writers, ranging from Georgia O'Keefe to the British novelist D. H. Lawrence, but it wasn't the hip mecca that it is today. Most residents were blue-collar Latinos, Native Americans, and whites who didn't take kindly to the long-haired flower children establishing desert communes and otherwise filtering into the area, chasing aquarian-tinged pleasure and enlightenment. The cultural wars of the era raged. It was the straights against the hippies, the two sides colliding in the high-desert peyote lands around Taos. As a long-haired skinny kid with a mustache, I was automatically sorted into the countercultural camp.

One day I was out running the highway—a 12-mile tempo run, my longest training run thus far—and saw some action up ahead: a carful of locals hassling a female long-haired hitchhiker. They were giving her a very hard time. As I ran closer—there was no place else to go, just one ribbon of highway, with the sagebrush flats spilling away on both sides of the road—I saw the guys pulling the girl into the car, the girl fighting wildly. What was I supposed to do about it—a 140-pound runner, not even wearing a shirt? But before I could think, I was banging on the roof of the car, yelling, "I see you guys, I know who you are! I have your license number!"

Which was true—they were a crew of brothers who lived near my parents' place. The guys looked up, obviously pissed that some pencil-necked long-haired jogger had the affront to spoil their party and bang on the roof of their rig. They let go of the girl and zeroed in on me. I got the hell out of there, booking away from the highway across the desert at a dead sprint. The guys snarled and swore behind me as they gave chase. It must have looked like a pack of Yosemite Sams chasing the Road Runner. I might have laughed if I hadn't been terrified. I ran into a gas station/grocery where I was friendly with the owner. The storekeeper had a shotgun behind the counter, and he brought it out to scare off my pursuers.

The guys drove away, telling me the same thing I had told them: "We see you, asshole; we know where you live."

A bizarre, week-long war ensued, one that engaged my entire family and one that finally, in characteristically twisted fashion, got my father to support my running. The morning after my confrontation with the locals, Dr. Sam went out to his truck and found the tires slashed. The family dogs had been poisoned. My brother-in-law Peter Blake, Ruth's husband, and I spent the next night sitting up on the roof, holding rifles, waiting for the men to return.

My enraged father, meanwhile, was clearly delighted to be going to war. With his .38-caliber pistol in his lap—the same handgun that he had carried around West Virginia, ostensibly "to kill snakes"—he drove behind me on my training runs. He wasn't really interested in protecting me or supporting my athletic career: I think he just wanted to shoot somebody. Dr. Sam was almost disappointed when the men's mother stepped in and called a halt to the absurd but dead-serious feud.

✦ ✦ ✦

Despite the turmoil and transitions, I still sensed I was breaking new ground with my training, and I felt increasingly confident that I was on the right track. I decided to give my running career a year and see how far it would take me.

The Olympic Games were slated for Munich, Germany, in

September 1972. After talking to Coach Giegengack and given my progress over the last few months, making the Olympic team didn't seem like an unrealistic long-term goal. But I had already learned that the process, the daily feedback from my experiment in self-coaching, was more important than the result. The question was, where could the experiment continue and how could I pay for it?

My stars lined up again. Fate drew me to Florida.

7

Intervals

At first glance—and even on second and third glance—Gainesville, Florida, would seem the opposite of an ideal running locale such as Taos, New Mexico, and one of the last places in the world you'd expect to form the seedbed for a flowering in American distance running and, eventually, for the first worldwide running boom. Located in the pancake-flat pine forest of central Florida, Gainesville was steamy and hot, nearly insufferable during the summer. The city wasn't near a major airport and, except for hosting the annual Florida Relays, wasn't a major destination on the national track circuit. Gainesville was home to the University of Florida, where football ruled. But the warmth that oppressed in the summer permitted year-round training—you could run in a T-shirt in January—and the cost of living was dirt cheap. The university featured a good Tartan Track and other training amenities. Most important, Gainesville had Jack Bacheler and Jimmy Carnes.

We have already met Jack, who, besides being the top 10,000-meter runner in the United States, was a budding world-class entomologist who would later do groundbreaking work as a professor and head of the agricultural extension service at North Carolina

State University. Despite his unassuming nature, he drew people to him because of his generosity and, for fellow runners, his encyclopedic knowledge of the practical aspects of the sport. Enrolled in a doctorate program at the university, Jack had established a training base in Gainesville, where he connected with Jimmy Carnes.

Jimmy was the head track coach at the University of Florida. He produced good teams and loved the sport, but he was no expert on the technique of any event and didn't pretend to be. Jimmy was an impresario, organizer, and logistical genius (Jimmy would later be chosen as head coach of the 1980 US Olympic track-and-field team, which did not compete in Moscow due to the United States–led boycott). He communicated a sense of fun and possibility to his athletes and reached out to anyone who shared his passion for track and field. Jimmy sensed immediately that Jack was a true believer and authentic talent. There was nothing Jimmy could teach him about training, but he could provide material support. Jack had finished his NCAA eligibility, and although he couldn't run for the University of Florida team, Jimmy helped him anyway. He founded the Florida Track Club (FTC), naming himself as coach and Jack as the club's charter member.

Others soon followed. The American distance-running community was a small tightly knit group. Jack spread the word about Gainesville's warm winter weather, decent facilities, supportive coach, and most importantly the cheap rents. Olympic steeplechase hopeful Barry Brown and his wife came down from upstate New York. Marty Liquori, one of the world's best milers, second only to Jim Ryun among American middle-distance runners, moved south from New Jersey. An Atlanta native, 10,000-meter stand-out, and future famed proponent of the run-walk system for the marathon, Jeff Galloway, lived in Tallahassee but trained with the FTC. John

Parker, the future novelist and a champion Southeast Conference miler, stayed on in Gainesville after graduating from Florida. While following various academic and professional pursuits, these guys all trained together at the University of Florida field house. The word on the circuit was that something special was happening in Gainesville. When Jack contacted me in Taos, where I was being chased by rowdies, dealing with my psychotic father, and laying cement for the foundation of a house addition, I was more than ready to accept his invitation. Working with Kenny Moore and Steve Prefontaine during the previous summer had convinced me of the enormous benefits of elite-level, like-minded training partners.

I flew back to New York and with my brother-in-law Ken drove down the eastern seaboard to Florida. I was a young starving artist practicing a sport that few Americans cared about, but I was on the right track. I was pursuing my destiny full-throat, batting down the highway with the window open and the radio blasting. I was 22 years old and on my way to Florida.

I hit Gainesville, and Jimmy and Jack got me oriented. Jack was married, and he and his wife, Jean, had their own student apartment. I threw in with John Parker. John had enrolled at the university law school for cover, for a fallback position, but like the rest of us, his passion was running. John also had his art—he was a nascent fiction writer. He invited me to move in with him. We shared a windowless chamber behind the equipment room in the university field house. At least the room was air-conditioned. We joked that we lived in a refrigerator, but that didn't matter because our true home was the track.

John was a miler, I was a distance runner, but we hammered the same intervals, building our speed. Jack often joined us. When we weren't training, John and I banged around town on his 50cc motorcycle. This was the spring of 1970. Most American campuses were on the verge of revolt, but things were relatively quiet at the University of Florida, where the FTC was quietly preparing for another kind of revolution.

I loved being part of this group, having consistent training partners who shared my point of view and my sense of responsibility toward the sport. The guys at the FTC wordlessly agreed to share the hard labor of pacing. We would try to tear each other's throats out during hard days, go easy on the easy days, and when the work was done, we had a blast together. It was like those summer workouts with Pre, but now they were available on a daily basis.

Most of us were preparing for the national outdoor track-and-field championships in June. Because Jack was the defending champion in the 10,000, the Amateur Athletic Union (AAU) sent him an airline ticket to fly to the meet in Bakersfield, California—a long way from Florida. Jack's expenses were covered, but what about the rest of us? Jimmy got working on it, discovering that he could cash in Jack's full-fare ticket and use it to buy two or three discount tickets. Would Jack be willing to forego his comfortable nonstop ride to help out his teammates? Of course he would. It wasn't even a question, and that attitude was emblematic of the spirit of the FTC—Jimmy Carnes's resourcefulness, Jack Bacheler's generosity.

Out in Bakersfield four of us packed into one small hotel room, but we didn't care. Pre was at the meet, running the 3-mile, having traveled down from Eugene, where he had just finished his freshman year at the University of Oregon. The week before, at the NCAA championships in Des Moines, Pre had slashed open his foot on a shard of broken glass at a motel swimming pool. But that didn't stop him from competing at the nationals in Bakersfield. He finished the race with his shoe full of blood, adding another chapter to his growing legend.

Jack Bacheler and I also ran that 3-mile race. Kicking past four other guys on the final turn, I covered the last 440 yards in 54.9; I had never run a stand-alone quarter-mile that fast, let alone one at the end of a 3-mile race. I prevailed over a field that included at least four sub-4-minute milers to win my first national championship in 13:24.2. At the end of the race, I looked up at the time, accepted the handshakes of the other guys, but I almost felt as if I were watching myself, as if it wasn't really happening. Where was all this success coming from? On the one hand I knew how hard I had worked—all those searing intervals, all those 140-mile weeks. On the other hand it seemed like magic.

I had the ability to run fast when I was tired. That was my only physical talent, the one thing that set me apart. I could stand at a distance from my pain, draw a sort of energy from it. Partly this was due to the diligence of my training, partly it was due to my efficient stride and my ability to run at 92 percent of my VO_2 max, and partly it was due to the savage boyhood beatings I'd received from my father: I had already learned to ride my pain.

The magic continued the next day when Jack and I shared a win in the 6-mile with a time of 27:24.0. The effort felt as easy as a Gainesville training run. The previous September I had been a medical-school dropout. Now, in June, I was a two-time national champion.

That success reinforced what I'd been doing in Gainesville, and I returned to Florida with renewed energy and focus. I lived in the refrigerator with Parker, banged around town with him on the motorbike, and stuck to my simple but brutal—and brutally satisfying—training routine. I would do intervals with Parker and whoever else was around the track and then log my long runs with Jack. The hard runs were run hard, and the easy runs at a conversational pace: If someone had to pause once to draw an extra breath, we were moving too fast. I trained at 11:30 a.m. and 3:30 p.m., as consistent as the Florida sun rising over the Atlantic and setting in the Gulf of Mexico. Barry Brown would lead a group run starting from the parking lot next to the stadium every afternoon. Jack Bacheler ran at daybreak at 6 a.m., but I wasn't a morning person; most mornings I trained alone. I just ran. No weights or strength work, no stretching or flexibility exercises, an ice bath on occasion but never any massage therapy or chiropractics. That fall, the FTC won the team title at the national cross-country championships up in New York City. I was the individual winner—my third national championship—and Jack finished second.

We didn't know we were living in a golden age; we thought we were just out there grinding. I loved hanging out with John Parker. We would go out and drink beer and engage in these amazing freewheeling discussions in which we'd challenge each other regarding all manner of political and philosophical concepts. When we got tired of all that, John, a native southern boy, would get a little down and dirty. On Thursday nights we'd gather at Barry Brown's house to watch TV, because he was the supposed grown-up of the club and the only one of us who owned a set.

But mostly we ran. We shared the same philosophy and code of honor, taking the good times with the bad, trading off the lead during intervals. On hard days we would be at each other's throats, and on long runs, moving at that conversational pace, we would tell each other everything (although I breathed not a word about my father; at that point I still couldn't admit the truth to myself). We shared hotel rooms and rides to meets. None of us had any money. There were no appearance fees or shoe contracts or prize winnings, with all their attendant anxieties and jealousies. We truly wished the best for one another. We were young guys tucked away in a hot, distant corner of the country, trying to figure out this new thing.

By necessity, running formed only one part of our lives. After a workout, Jack would go to his bug studies, Barry to his insurance business, Liquori to the shoe and apparel outfit he was starting up with Jimmy Carnes (which eventually grew into the hugely successful Athletic Attic chain), and John Parker to his law-school studies and fiction writing.

At first I didn't have an outside interest, and I missed the intellectual stimulation; I missed learning. I had to do something else besides train. Following Parker's example, I took the LSATs and got admitted to the university law school. Jimmy Carnes, bless his heart, made sure I qualified for in-state tuition: just $240 a quarter. All I had to do was buy law books. Meanwhile, I conducted a long-distance romance with Louise Gilliland, a woman I had met out in Boulder during one of my altitude-training sojourns, who was studying to be a librarian. Louise eventually joined me in Gainesville. By this time Parker had gotten married, so the four of us lived in a house together, sharing the rent. Louise would make a few bucks babysitting Barry Brown's kids.

Parker and I continued to work the intervals together. Among our group, John might have been the least talented natural athlete. He worked as hard as the rest of us, but he had only the one event, the mile, and he couldn't break down past the 4:06 range. John's true gift, of course, was for the word. In his brilliant novel *Once a Runner,* he captured the essence of who we were and what we sought. I loved talking with John. We would bat around a topic as if it were a balloon we were keeping in the air.

It seemed as if there was plenty of time for everything. No false modesty, but after the rigors of Yale, I found law school at Florida to be relatively easy. I learned that I didn't have to spend overkill hours in the library to succeed in my studies. I would go to class at 9 a.m., hit another class at 10; then at 11, I would book out for a 9-mile run. I attended a third class around noon, followed by a few hours of studying and my 3:30 p.m. workout. Looking back, it does seem like a golden age.

8

26.2

I started law school in the spring of 1971, one year before the '72 Olympic summer. The Pan American Games that summer in Cali, Colombia, served as a precursor to Munich. The US trials for Pan Am coincided with the Amateur Athletic Union (AAU) championships in Eugene, Oregon, in June. By this time I'd gotten to be friends with Kenny Moore—we competed against each other often and trained together whenever our schedules meshed. Kenny, a born and bred Oregon Duck, never joined the Florida Track Club (FTC), but with his energy, talent, sense of honor, and layered intelligence—if John Parker became the sport's signature novelist, then Kenny, in his later work for *Sports Illustrated*, developed into running's premier journalist—he would have fit in perfectly.

Kenny advised that, going into the qualifying rounds for an international competition, it was always smart to have a back-up event. Say you turned an ankle or caught the flu or ate some tainted meat and had to sit out your main event; if you had punched your ticket in another race, you would still be getting on the airplane. My central event was the 10,000. I was also the defending national champ in the 5000, but my long-term prospects at that distance weren't the greatest. My strength lay in the longer stuff, distances at which I could ride my pain. For my back-up event, I chose the marathon.

Back at Yale, Bob Giegengack predicted that I had the potential to be a first-rate distance runner. I realized that my particular skill set—the ability to hold a fast pace, surge at a harder pace, then return to the hard baseline—was ideally suited for the marathon. I also knew that the speed I'd built on the track would set me apart from other marathoners who typically lacked distinguished track credentials; they turned to 26.2 because they were too slow to win shorter races. But the marathon, at that point, was largely an unknown continent. The distance was foreboding, running's equivalent of the white whale (indeed, one of the most startling transformations of our time is that today, every year, hundreds of thousands of normal citizens routinely run the marathon, a feat that 50 years ago was akin to climbing Mount Everest). You didn't race the marathon; you survived it. At least that was the common wisdom at the time. I thought there might be a better approach.

My own direct experience with the event had started earlier, in 1968, right after my parents had moved out west to New Mexico. I was out there visiting when the US Olympic Marathon Trials were taking place in Alamosa, Colorado, not too far from Taos. My brother Chris and I drove over to take a look. In those days anyone could enter the trials, and nobody cared much about race security. It was just a couple dozen or so skinny maniacs running, and not that many more spectators watching.

On a whim, I decided to enter the marathon. At the Adams State University gym I signed up with the race director, Buddy Edelin, who once held the American record in the marathon. I then looked up Amby Burfoot, who earlier that year had won the Boston Marathon. I needed some racing flats and thought that Amby might lend me a pair. Amby graciously lent me the shoes. The trouble was, they were size 9, and I wore a 10 and a half. But I wore them anyway.

Amby and I lined up at the start together, and off we went, falling in with a lead pack of around eight runners. Around the 5-mile mark, Bill Clark, winner of that year's 10,000 meters in the first Olympic Trials, looked at me and said, "Who are you?"

"I'm here with Amby," I replied.

At around the marathon's halfway point, which was farther than I'd ever run at the time, my blistered feet did me in, and I was forced to stop. Amby dropped out at around the same point, around 3 miles from the finish line on the loop course. We watched the three qualifiers go by: George Young, Kenny Moore, and Ron Daws. I had learned what the marathon felt like if you hadn't prepared, if you didn't go in with a plan.

My painful apprenticeship continued at those Pan Am trials, the first marathon I ran seriously. My mentor and guide was Kenny Moore, who, after the Olympic Trials in Alamosa, had run the distance at the Olympic Games in Mexico City in 1968 and who had finished second in the Fukuoka Marathon in Japan the year before, setting an American record for the distance. Kenny and I shared the lead at the 22-mile mark, but I was hurting. I was tapped out, with suppurating blisters and athletic tape flapping off the pair of Tiger trainers I had lashed together to carry me through the race. I was learning firsthand about the mysteries and cruelties of the region that lay beyond 20 miles, the notorious wall, the point at which glycogen stores bottom out and your brain starts sending bizarre, sabotaging messages. It was my first visit to this neighborhood. I turned to Kenny and complained, "Why couldn't

Pheidippides (the Athenian who ran from Marathon to Athens to announce victory in the battle against the Persians, inspiring the modern running event) have died at 22 miles?"

Kenny gave a tight little smile and took off, winning the race in 2:16:49. I came in second, running on fumes, about a minute later. My first thought on crossing the marathon finish line was, "Oh, God! Now I have to run another one of these!" My pain notwithstanding, I had secured my back-up plan. Indeed, although I hardly realized it at the time, I had found my destiny.

✦ ✦ ✦

That summer at the Pan American Games in Cali, Columbia, I won the 10,000 meters in 28:50.83, a decent time considering we were competing under a broiling sun at more than a 4000-foot altitude. Now, on the meet's final day, came my supposed back-up event, the marathon. Kenny and I jumped to the lead, where we were joined by a Columbian runner named Álvero Ernesto Mejía, who had won the 1971 Boston Marathon the previous April. The three of us were booming along until, at the 15-mile mark, I got nailed by a blast of the *turistas*. I had to peel off the road to take care of business. It didn't take long, but by the time I jumped back in the race, Kenny and Mejía were about 150 yards in front of me, specks on my windshield.

I set my jaw and threw down one of the surges I'd been practicing during my interval sessions, and before long I had caught them. "I'm back!" I chirped to Kenny. Mejía turned to me and his eyes got as big as saucers. My recovery unnerved him, and he quickly dropped out of contention. Now it was Kenny and me, knocking down the miles as if we were on a training run back in the States.

I felt full of running this time; I was getting the hang of this. The territory beyond mile 20 no longer seemed hostile.

We passed 21, and the sun was hammering, but we were hanging in. This was all right. I wasn't going to bonk. Maybe Kenny and I could dead-heat together, share the victory. But I glanced over at him and saw that something was wrong. He was pale and shaky. "Kenny," I said, "you stopped sweating."

Dangerously dehydrated, Kenny slowed to a stagger. A fierce, unyielding competitor, he was so glad to see an ambulance person waving at him that he submitted to their cooling ministrations without complaint. He would later say that he felt lucky to have been pulled off the course.

I carried on to the finish, feeling bad for my friend but reveling in this hospitable new country. I won the race in 2:22:40, another good performance given the altitude. My two Pan Am gold medals put me on the international map. Representatives from the Fukuoka Marathon invited me to run their race in December.

I accepted right away. I was suddenly hooked on the marathon. After three meetings with the monster, I felt as if I had made friends with him—or at least we had arrived at an amicable, productive, working relationship. I knew I could survive—even thrive—over those final 6 miles, despite the fact that, strictly speaking, I couldn't really prepare for them. I had already discovered that, for me, it was counterproductive to exceed 20 miles for a long training run. Because if you ran long on Sunday, you had to recover on Monday before logging a hard interval session on Tuesday. If you went over 20 on your long run, you would burn into your physical capital and have to take an extra day of recovery, or even worse sacrifice some quality in your speed workout, which would propel you on a downward spiral.

The body starts to break down past 20 miles, and you have to save that breakdown for a race. All you can do (short of cheating with performance-enhancing drugs) is make yourself as uncomfortable as possible during your intervals and long runs, so that, instead of crashing, you can work with the pain that comes beyond 20 on race day. It takes a lot of thought, effort, and trial and error to bake the cake right. I seemed to have found a recipe that worked.

The challenge of those final 6.2 miles was primarily mental. What do you think about? Anything that gets you down the road. Some marathoners dissociate and fantasize; others lock in to the moment. In my case, I told myself that those final miles in a marathon race were no more painful than the last 400-repeat during a hard training day. If I could hang in during training, I could do the same while competing. At the Pan Am marathon, moreover, I experienced the boost you get from finishing in a stadium, in front of a sizable crowd. That felt better than a road finish. There was something about the focus of a stadium, the angle between the track and spectators. If I got a bump from the stadium finish in Cali, imagine the jolt from the Olympic Stadium in Munich.

I could handle the long, grinding effort of marathon training. The challenge was physical, emotional, and intellectual; I perceived the marathon as a discipline I could learn. I did not die at the end. I did not fall apart. It hurt, but I could deal with it. Day by day, mile by mile, I even learned to get on top of it. As the year 1971 drew to a close, I'd found a new way to ride my pain.

9

Eternal Vigilance

At the time, Fukuoka and Boston were the only two major annually held marathons in existence. Among the elite international running community, Fukuoka had far more prestige than Boston did. Due to Cold War travel restrictions, Eastern Bloc runners couldn't travel freely to the United States; Boston was largely the province of Americans, Japanese, and Finns. But the whole world could travel to Japan—the Russians and Eastern Europeans as well as Asians and Westerners. Other than the Olympic Marathon, Fukuoka was the only marathon that was truly global.

The race fell at an optimal slot in my calendar, early December, just one week after I had won the individual title at the 1971 national cross-country championships in San Diego. Safe to say, I was on a roll; everything was working at every distance. I flew to Hawaii, then on to Fukuoka, a resort sea town on one of Japan's southern islands. The race, tied in with the Bushido samurai code of discipline, stoicism, and self-sacrifice, had a long history and occupied a special place in Japanese culture. "We love the marathon," the race officials explained to me. "It is one event we can do well in despite our small physical stature." The Japanese took great pride in Sohn Kee-chung, who, despite being a Korean national, won the gold medal in the 1936 Olympic marathon while representing Japan. He remained a hero in that nation less than three decades removed from the devastation of the Second World War.

The organizers were very hospitable, and I loved the experience right from the start. The luxury hotel was all about design and efficiency rather than size, and not an inch of space was wasted in the doll-size guest rooms. The quilts were so thick that you almost disappeared when you lay down on them. The organizers took the invited athletes out for a tour of the racecourse. It was my first visit to Japan, and I liked it: For all its foreignness, the streets, the sidewalks, the trolley cars gave off a familiar vibe. I was wearing my running kit and shoes under my warm-ups. I had a plan. I asked the bus driver to drop me off 7 miles away from the hotel, which was adjacent to the finish line. The bus stopped, I slipped out of my sweats, and took off running at race pace. The other runners sat on the bus watching me, thinking, what the hell? Also . . . this guy is booking; he's got some wheels. It was part of my mind-game strategy. I guess I'd learned something from Dr. Sam.

Was I worried about getting lost in a strange country where I didn't know the language? Not really. I had carefully studied the landmarks on the outbound ride. On my run I kept to the sidewalks, thinking about the look on those other guys' faces as I stepped off the bus, the way my move had shaken them.

Race day came, and I enacted my secret plan. I hadn't even told Kenny about my scheme. As I've mentioned, up until this point the marathon was the white whale of track in particular, and the sporting world in general. Running 26.2 miles was perceived to be the province of near-lunatics. The aim was to survive the race, just endure the suffering, and whoever bore the most suffering on a given day would be the winner. There were no tactics to speak of; you just ran at a steady pace and tried to hold it. The winner was the guy who fell apart last. I respected the marathon—I had certainly felt its wrath during my first two races—but today I aimed to do more than survive.

The starting gun cracked, and we headed out into the teeth of a strong, steady gale off the North Pacific. It was an out-and-back course. You ran out about 15 miles along the beach, then you did a 180 and ran back home. The wind took a lot out of us during the first half, which also played into my plan. As we neared the turn-around point, I told Kenny, who was running beside me, "We turn that corner, all hell's gonna break loose."

We turned the corner, and I surged as if I were coming off the final turn of a track race. I floored it for 3 kilometers, and no one could go with me; the wind and the early pace had sapped them. They watched me go with the same expression as when I'd gotten out of the bus a few days earlier. I surged through that stretch at about a 4:40 per mile pace and then throttled back to a pace just over 5:00 a mile, the pace the lead pack was running before my surge. That gave me about a 30-second lead, but the common wisdom held that my gambit had been self-immolating. By expending all that energy so early, the thinking went, I wouldn't be able to hold that previous leader's pace, and eventually the pack would reel me in and swallow me.

But I was coming at it from the opposite direction—how hard would those guys have to go to catch up with me? All I had to do was hold my pace at just under maximum effort, ride my pain, and in training I had proven that I could do that. Now, I'd just do it again. I maintained my 30-second lead over Akio Usami from Japan, the defending champion. I won the race in 2:12:50, a Personal Record (PR) for me but still well off Derek Clayton's 2:08:33 world record. I never ran for time; I ran for the win, and today had been windy. The relatively slow time worked to my advantage. The experts could regard my performance as something of a fluke. The question remained: Would my surge-and-recover strategy and track-based tactics work in the Olympic Marathon?

I was going to find out. Heading into the Olympic year 1972, I thought of myself primarily as a marathoner. My odds for victory improved as a race grew longer. I knew I lacked the finishing speed to contend for a medal in the 5000 meters. My mile PR was 4:06, and to make it to the medal podium in the 5-K, you really needed sub-4-minute-mile speed. However, not many of the marathon contenders could compete with my mile speed. For the most part, their mantra was miles, their primary goal endurance. One exception was Kenny Moore, who owned a 4:03.2 PR for the mile. His training with Bowerman was similar to mine: the same twice-weekly short intervals and long intervals. Kenny differed from me in that, physiologically, he could handle long training runs exceeding 20 miles. Every 10 days, Kenny would log a long run starting at 25 miles and build up to 35.

By contrast, I realized that, for me, elite marathon training was paradoxical—in order for me to succeed on the 26.2-mile road, I had to base my training on the 400-meter track. Indeed, even though I was shifting my focus from the 5000 and 10,000 to the marathon, I didn't change my training at all. I followed the same fundamentals as before: a weekly 20-mile run with at least 10 miles run at sub-5-minute pace and 100 more easy-paced miles logged through the remainder of the week; two weekly speed workouts on the track, at the end of which, if I had done them right, had someone held a gun to my head, saying, run another quarter or I'll shoot, again I would have said go ahead and shoot because it would hurt less.

I knew that following this formula presented my best chance for winning a medal, but the routine also settled my head and heart. My childhood had taught me to be eternally vigilant, and vigilance leads to consistency. You could set your watch by my workouts. I never missed a day.

+ + +

After Fukuoka I spent the winter of 1971 to 1972 in Gainesville, fine-tuning my routine. In April I broke camp in the East to go to the mountains of the West. The benefits of altitude training were just starting to filter down to American runners. When Kip Keino had decisively beaten Jim Ryun in the mile at the Mexico City Games, we started to see the writing on the wall. Runners who grew up at mile-high-plus altitude in the Rift Valley of Kenya and Ethiopia had a huge advantage over athletes who lived and trained at sea level. Keino, along with the gold medal marathoners Abebe Bikila and Mamo Wolde, formed a vanguard; soon the East Africans would be coming in droves.

The only way to compete with them—at least legally—was to boost your red-blood cell volume by living and training for periods of time at or above around 5,000-foot altitude. We were just starting to experiment with the technique to figure out the best combinations. For example, during a spell at altitude, do you spend all your time up high, or do you come down to lower elevations at specific times for speed workouts that are impossible to log in the thin mountain air?

Fortunately, I had already established contacts in the West, had some experience training in the Rockies, and had an idea of what I wanted to accomplish from a physiological perspective. Also, I had confidence—the confidence of youth and confidence from my recent performances. I had been coaching myself for two years now without a serious mistake or misstep, no injuries despite the intense workload, no crash-and-burns during a race. Feeling loose and in sync, in February I wrote to Bob Parker, general manager of Vail Associates in Colorado. I explained who I was, that I'd trained at the Taos ski mountain with good results, and so on. Could Vail help me out? Parker said sure, no one stayed in the condos in April; come on out and we'll comp you in a unit.

I traveled to Colorado with Louise and my friends from Florida in tow—when one of us in the club got lucky, we always shared our good fortune. On our way out there, Louise and I stayed at then Colorado Secretary of State Mary Estill Buchanan's house, where we had dinner with her and Bob Lang, the inventor of the Lang Ski Boot. Lang kindly offered us the use of his duplex in Vail, and we accepted. Louise and I stayed there with Jack Bacheler, his wife, Jean, and their tiny son, Matt, while Jeff Galloway stayed at the Valhalla condominium Parker had arranged for us. Jeff drove over to train and hang with us in an old Volvo with floorboards so rotted out you could see the road rushing by underneath. We spent a fine few weeks hammering the high-country miles. There was a golf course at Vail but not many golfers, and we had the place to ourselves, running tempo workouts over the smooth green fairways with the granite peaks jutting all around and the sunshine glinting off the water-hazard lakes and the crashing snowmelt rivers.

That spring I internalized the live-high, run-low philosophy. At 8,000 feet, Vail was too high to run intervals fast enough to do us any good, so twice a week we'd drive down to Boulder to run intervals on the track at the University of Colorado. Day after day we hit that sweet spot, every workout paying off. At night we'd drink beer in the local taverns, playing Derek and the Dominos' "Layla" over and over on the jukebox.

Sometimes I felt so good, so strong, that I almost scared myself. One week I ran a total of 180 miles. Two runs a day weren't enough for me, so I ran three times, morning, noon, and night. Even on relatively easy weeks we never went below 120, which was like running 140 at sea level. From 1970 to 1980, my training log averages 17 miles a day, seven days a week, 52 weeks in every golden year.

10

Summer Days at Hayward Field

After that successful altitude-training stint in Vail, we sailed on full of confidence to the 1972 US Olympic Trials in Eugene, Oregon. I say "we" because even though the loneliness of the long-distance runner is more than a cliché—over the last mile, on that final lap, no matter how close you are to your teammates, every runner is on his or her own—I felt part of a vibrant American running community, one that encompassed not just the Florida Track Club (FTC), and, increasingly, not only Olympic-level athletes.

Catalyzed by the seminal 1967 book *Jogging* by Bill Bowerman, who had been influenced in turn by Arthur Lydiard, the great New Zealand coach, the fitness running movement was starting to build across the nation. *Aerobics,* a book by Dr. Ken Cooper, a Dallas cardiologist who had run the Boston Marathon, lent scientific credence to running for health. Out in California, a young runner from Kansas named Bob Anderson had started to publish a magazine called *Runner's World*.

There was a sudden surge of interest in running on both coasts, in Gainesville and Boston and New York, in Los Angeles and Eugene and Seattle. The general activism of the times joined with this movement; running was emerging as another expression of the counterculture, a means of personal and societal transformation. A crop of exceptional coaches was on hand to mold a rising cadre of elite runners: Bowerman at Oregon, Giegengack at Yale, Jumbo Elliot at Villanova, Bill Squires with the Greater Boston Track Club.

Bowerman and Giegengack also served as key advocates to the Amateur Athletic Union (AAU), the sport's increasingly sclerotic governing body, which, too often, put its own interests in front of those of the athletes. For instance, if Gieg could send every Yale kid who qualified to the NCAA championship meet, even if he had no hope of scoring any points, why couldn't the AAU do the same for all athletes meeting the more stringent requirements for the US Olympic Trials? Bowerman and Gieg could make these kinds of arguments to the officials without threatening them. They made the case that we, the athletes, weren't wild-eyed radicals out to destroy the system. We just wanted to reform the organization and bring it into the modern era.

Kenny Moore and I had gotten to be good friends, so he and I stayed with a couple that Kenny knew in Eugene. There wasn't much choice; we had no funding for lodging. The AAU didn't even provide per diem meal money, and as I recall, we had to pay for our own travel to Oregon. Nonetheless, those were halcyon days for the sport. Across the board, the United States had the best track team in the world. The sprinters continued the long tradition of American dominance. In the middle distances, the miler Jim Ryun and the 800-meter runner Dave Wottle were putting up world-class times. In the longer distances, we were demonstrating medal potential at the FTC; Kenny was consistently one of the world's best marathoners, and here in Eugene Steve Prefontaine had boosted the University of Oregon program, already renowned under Bowerman's guidance, to an even higher level.

Most exceptional high school runners level out or go downhill during their first year or two in college. But not Pre. He had taken that phenomenal 2-mile record he set as a senior in high school at Coos Bay and used it as a springboard. He just kept getting faster, and the style of his running was just as impressive as its substance (indeed, with Pre, there was no gap between substance and style, which was the key to his appeal). He was always pushing, always running from the front, belting his guts out at every race, and it didn't hurt that he was movie-star handsome, with long blonde hair and the recent addition of a Sundance Kid mustache (around this time I grew my own drooping hippie mustache as well). Pre had electrified the Eugene running community, which was already famous for the passionate, knowledgeable fans packing Hayward Field for every track competition.

Per my custom, I had a busy meet in front of me. The trials followed the same schedule as the Games, with the 10,000 meters taking place during the first few days of the 10-day-long competition and the marathon trials scheduled on the final day (only the men's; there was no women's marathon until 1984). That was the last time that the marathon trials took place during the track trials; from '76 on the marathon trials took place months earlier, giving marathoners more time to recover and prepare for the Games. I didn't have that benefit in '72, but the workload didn't faze me. Starting at Mount Hermon, I always competed in more than one event at every meet, and I'd always been able to recover quickly from all-out efforts. I could race the 5000 and 10,000 on consecutive days and run them both well. Now, in Eugene, the marathon would be my priority, and the 10 would form my hedge. In fact, I planned to use the 10 as a tool to sharpen my marathon performance.

The task wouldn't be easy. There was a small group of very talented distance runners competing for the Olympic spots. Besides being fine runners, they were also dimensional and well-educated gentlemen; ironically, they were classic amateur athletes, examples of the Avery Brundage–era model we sought to overturn. Jeff Galloway had graduated from Wesleyan, Kenny had earned an MFA in creative writing at Oregon, and Jack had earned his doctorate in entomology.

So all of these currents were swirling and commingling at the Olympic Trials in Eugene in June 1972. Long-haired girls in tight bell-bottom jeans smiling as we ran past on the trails through Amazon Park and along the fir-shaded banks of the Willamette. Pre's army of fans roaring as he stepped to the starting line at Hayward Field. There was almost a rock festival atmosphere, with no distinct line between the performers and the fans. We were all joined in this new project, the aquarian vibe detracting not a whit from the rigor and excellence of the running, jumping, and throwing; in fact, each realm strengthened the other. It was hard to grasp, harder to put into words, but you walked around in a sort of giddy daze. We all knew we had been drawn into something special.

The atmosphere at Hayward felt electric as I toed the line for the qualifying heat in the 10,000. I had to remind myself not to get lost in it. Draw energy but don't lose my edge. Stay with the mantra, go with the plan. I basically trotted through the semifinal, winning my heat in 29:07.4, content merely to qualify for the final, which I won in 28:35.6, still running under control. I had punched my ticket to Munich. A few years earlier, I was a scrawny, frightened little kid running across Middletown in a pair of low-top PF Flyers. Now Dr. Sam's son was a national champion and an Olympian.

Making the Munich team in the 10, during the first event of the trials, took the pressure off for the marathon. Kenny and I had the two fastest qualifying times by a good margin, and there was a certain security in that. We knew our competition, knew whom we were dealing with. In the marathon, performance-enhancing drugs weren't much of an issue in 1972. Some guy we never heard of wasn't going to drop out of the sky, as would be the case in 1976 and, sadly, in all the Olympic Games thereafter.

Kenny and I ran together the entire race. We went out fast and quickly separated from the rest of the field. As the miles unreeled, we took turns setting the pace and breaking the headwinds. We didn't have a set plan. We just worked according to our intuitive sense of pace, moving back and forth, sharing the responsibility of the lead. All we needed was a top-three finish to make the team, and that was in the bag. It almost felt like a dance, or perhaps a moderately hard, long training run. We crossed the line together in a 2:15:57 tie. That race may have been the most enjoyable marathon of my career—if such a tepid adjective could ever be used in describing any attack on the white whale of a distance.

Meanwhile, a more dramatic scene was building just in back of us. Jack Bacheler, my good friend from Gainesville and the mentor and guiding spirit of the FTC, hadn't been faring well at the trials. In the 10,000 meters, his specialty, Jack had finished a disappointing fourth, trailing me, a runner from Oregon named Jon Anderson, and Jeff Galloway, thus narrowly missing one of the three Olympic berths. Now it appeared that the same thing would happen in the marathon. Jack and Jeff were fighting it out for third place, but Jack was clearly struggling. Although he had the third spot locked up, Jeff, knowing he already had his

Munich berth secured in the 10, slowed down over the final mile, letting Jack earn the Olympic spot he so richly deserved. Jeff Galloway's sacrifice seemed to exemplify the very best of the entire Olympic experience.

+ + +

If you go to a US Olympic Trials meet now, it seems that half the crowd consists of parents and family members who have traveled from all corners of the nation to watch their children compete in what is often the crowning moments of their athletic careers and one of the unforgettable experiences of their lives. So did my parents make the relatively short trip from New Mexico to watch me qualify in two events for the Munich Games? No way. Indeed, I had had no contact with my father since 1970. My father had stayed away from every race I had ever run, and he wasn't going to break that streak now. Nor did I expect him to. I had established a new family: Louise, whom I'd married in 1970, and the tribe of runners in and around the track of Hayward Field.

Louise was there to watch me run, and I watched from the infield as Pre, the crown prince of our extended royal running family, duked it out with George Young to win the 5000 in an American record time of 13:22.8. The crowd went wild. I didn't give my parents a thought. Why look back at the night when the morning is opening all around you?

Now, looking back through the decades, I can recognize the depth of my denial. I knew what my father was up to. I knew that while I was circling the track in the sunshine at Hayward Field, my siblings remained under attack back in Taos. But you get really good at hiding it, not thinking about it. I never even told Louise about my childhood. It wasn't that I was ashamed—at least not only because of my shame. I had been so singlemindedly goal-oriented for so long, so attached to routine and plan and schedule—so committed to the structures freeing me to move both physically and emotionally—that if I had told Louise the truth, I'm not sure I could have dealt with the consequences: all of the anger, all of the guilt, and all of the fear.

The truth was that, at age 24 and on my way to the Olympic Games, I remained viscerally afraid of Dr. Sam. When you learn to be afraid at an early age, the fear never dies. You really believe that the person you're afraid of—especially when that person is the one who is supposed to love and protect you—retains the power to destroy you. And I'm not just speaking metaphorically. Moreover, in 1972, my father's power and persona remained at its height. Who would believe the private horror generated by a man of such extravagant public virtue? Finally, my private pain and guilt also formed the source—at least one source—of my gift for the marathon. I had learned to isolate my anguish and channel it into the miles.

So the 1972 Olympic Trials in Eugene passed in a blue-gold dream and exactly according to my steadily evolving plan. My marathon had even seemed dreamlike; I had run unchallenged, sharing the lead with my good friend. I had earned two berths in the 20th Olympic Games. I had ascended to a new level. Now how could I climb to the next one?

11

The Happy Games

I had a plan, which had been building for more than a year. The plan accelerated during my experiences at the Fukuoka Marathon and Olympic Trials, and now, as the US Olympic track-and-field team traveled to Oslo, Norway, to train for a month before the Games, it was coming to term.

The month in Oslo was Bill Bowerman's idea. Bowerman's title was head coach of the American team, but he had the perspective to understand that he was really a facilitator. Except for Oregon athletes such as Pre, whose training he had helped to supervise previously, Bowerman wasn't about to meddle with any of our programs. Instead, he aimed to put us into position to succeed and to act as a broker between the athletes and the often clueless and self-serving suits of the US Olympic Committee and the International Olympic Committee.

The training camp in Oslo offered privacy and excellent training facilities—a first-rate running track and soft-surface trails around a lake. I knocked out my intervals and long runs, my hard days when I ran very hard and the easy days when, comparatively, I ran very easy. I hit my first workout at 11:30 a.m., when most other runners had long since wrapped up their morning work and were now either eating lunch or conking out for a nap, and my second just four hours later, at 3:30 p.m.; my teammates were impressed by my ability to recover so quickly. During this time, I continued to hatch my plan that was so simple in concept but difficult in execution: Similar to the marathon in Fukuoka, I was going to turn the Olympic Marathon into a track race.

If my training was geared toward any specific distance or event, it was actually the 5-K; I ran my intervals at the same volume, speed, and intensity as the middle-distance guys such as Pre and Marty Liquori. Competitively, however, my events were the marathon and the 10-K. I excelled at long distances off of 5-K training (that is, 5-K training with the added element of a weekly 20-mile run and weekly training mileage amounting to around 120). Now I doubled down on that seeming paradoxical scheme: Make myself as uncomfortable as possible during interval training, so I'd be as comfortable as possible during the marathon race.

For instance, for a given interval workout, instead of running 6×800 meters at a steady 2:10 per rep pace, I would vary my pace within each rep. I would run the first 200 meters relatively slowly, at a 2:12 pace, hammer the next 400 meters, and then run the final 200 at a recovery pace that was still faster than I'd run for the first 200. The goal was to learn to moderate and manage my pain over precise, predictable distances and to mimic the pattern of pacing I'd employ during the marathon race.

During the marathon I planned to run with the lead pack during the first part of the race, break away from the pack with a 3-mile surge, then dial back to a pace slower than my surge but faster than the pace at which I had run the early miles prior to the surge. If the plan worked as I hoped, I would open a lead that none of my opponents could challenge.

That was essentially the same strategy I'd employed at Fukuoka, slingshotting away from Kenny and from Akio Usami, then one of the top-ranked marathoners in the world, at the halfway point. In Munich, I decided, I would try to break the race open even earlier—at the 9-mile mark. Fukuoka had proven I could hold a lead for 13 miles; my work since then was preparing me to hold that lead—ride my pain—for about 17 miles.

Rather than regarding the 10,000 meters as a goal in itself, I approached it as a key building block of my marathon strategy. I knew I could hang in the 10 against guys like Lasse Viren of Finland and Emiel Puttemans of Belgium, but I lacked the sub-4-minute-mile speed that was necessary to keep contact with them when they made their late-race surges, or especially, their final-lap kicks. In short, I wasn't a medal contender in the 10. But at the same time, no other marathoner could come close to my speed for the distance. Put another way, I was the slowest runner in the top tier of the world's 10,000-meter runners but the fastest at that pivotal distance among the world's top marathoners.

Accordingly, during the marathon, I planned to exploit my 10-K speed to run mile 9 to mile 10 in 4:30, which was faster than some of my competitors' personal records (PRs) for a stand-alone mile. I would then cover mile 11 to 18 at a 4:50 pace—about 10 seconds a mile faster than the pace of the lead pack trailing me. Over the final 8 miles, if I just maintained a relatively comfortable 5-minute-mile pace, there should be no way that a rival could catch up with me. Moreover, I had closely studied the Munich Marathon course and noticed that it was full of twists and turns. If I got 200 meters ahead of the lead pack during my surge, the other guys wouldn't be able to see me. That would be a significant advantage; in any sort of footrace, it's always easier to run down prey that you have in your sights.

That was my strategy. I had laid the groundwork, and soon I would learn if I'd gotten it right. I told no one about the specifics of my scheme, not even Jack or Kenny. However, they could see what I was doing. In Oslo, I ran my 800s on the track where everybody logged their workouts. I knew I was in shape, because once a week I would run for 40 minutes at about 80 percent of my maximum perceived effort—about the pace I planned for my mid-race surge. During each of these timed runs, I covered more distance than on the previous session. By this time I was enjoying the intellectual exercise of self-coaching almost as much as the physical act of running. I had now been coaching myself for three years—since the middle of my junior year at Yale, when Gieg had given me the reins.

Midway through the month in Oslo, feeling increasingly confident that I'd been making the right decisions, I proposed another experiment. Having told Bowerman about my success with altitude training in New Mexico and most recently at Vail, I suggested that a stint of altitude would be beneficial now. Bill agreed and sent Kenny, Pre, and me up to the mountains near Lillehammer for a week. I'm not sure we got much physiological benefit from so short a stay, but we got a psychological boost. No other runners were making this sort of effort. We were doing absolutely everything we could to succeed. No runner in Munich was going to outwork or outthink us.

We returned to Oslo and, a full two weeks before the Games' opening ceremonies, broke camp and headed to Munich. That gave us ample time to acclimate to the surroundings and focus on the final stages of training. We immediately saw that the organizers had done a first-rate job of preparing for the Games, displaying their famous Teutonic competence and efficiency.

Just 25 years had passed since the end of the Second World War and all its Nazi-perpetrated horrors, and the West Germans carefully avoided any hint of repression. In fact, they branded their Olympics as "The Happy Games," accentuating bright colors and soaring, hopeful architecture. The goal was to contrast the event both from Hitler's 1936 Games in Berlin and from the gray starkness of present-day East Germany and the rest of the Soviet Bloc. The cold war was at its height in 1972, and the Munich Games served both as an interlude of truce and a tool that both sides exploited for propaganda. A light West German security footprint was part of that effort, a decision that would soon prove tragically misguided.

We had comfortable lodgings. The German organizers were thinking long-term when they built the athletes' village; after the Games, the dorms would become flats and apartments for the citizens of Munich. I was assigned a room in a large suite with several distance and middle-distance runners: Kenny Moore, Mike Manley, Steve Savage, Jon Anderson, and Dave Wottle. Dave and I were the only guys who weren't from Oregon or who didn't have strong ties to the state. Our suite was on the fourth floor. The bedrooms were arranged around a large central living area, and two wide doors opened out to a balcony that looked out over a parklike courtyard we shared with the other dorms in the housing complex. The running track and park trails were close at hand; we could roll out the back door of the building and just start running. The dining hall served a variety of good food, cafeteria-style, and lay just a hundred yards away, next door to the athletes' beer garden (I permitted myself a half-liter the night before my marathon, followed by plenty of water).

The first heat of the 10,000 meters was less than two weeks

away, but I resumed an ambitious training schedule; I was never much of a fan of tapering. I kept up my 11:30 a.m./3:30 p.m. routine, running 10 to 15 miles a day. I knocked out intervals on the track and traveled by metro to various points on the marathon course, aiming to run every mile to familiarize myself with the terrain. I made a special study of the English Garden, a large park in the manner of Central Park in New York City, and the grounds and buildings of Nymphenburg Palace, where I planned to launch my surge.

In the days before the opening ceremony, Louise and my sister Nanette arrived in Munich to see me run and watch other Olympic events. Many of the US athletes had been joined by their significant others. Kenny's wife, Bobbie Conlan, was on hand, as was Dave Wottle's recent bride. They were supposed to receive passes that would enable them to visit us in the fenced-in village, but the passes never materialized. We soon learned, however, that it was easy to doctor and forge our athletes' ID cards. For some reason the cards of equestrian competitors were especially easy to copy. With these fake documents the women could come and go as they pleased.

Louise's mother, Ernie, and her partner, Margaret, had rented an apartment in the city and Nanette and one of Louise's friends stayed with them. But Jan, Dave Wottle's wife, was on her own. After Dave won his gold medal in the 800 with a dramatic come-from-behind kick, wearing his signature white tennis cap, he brought Jan to stay in our unit. I had one of the larger bedrooms, so I gave them the space and, as I mentioned earlier, dragged my mattress out to the balcony. I slept soundly; with all the athletes in training, the village was quiet by 10 p.m., and the early risers never bothered me.

On the first day of track-and-field competition, I got busy with the 10,000 meters. Jeff Galloway and Jon Anderson, my US teammates, failed to make it into the final, but I ran 27:58 in my heat, an American record, the first sub-28 minute 10-K ever by an American, and I qualified for the final. Although encouraged by my performance, I still knew I had at best an outside shot at a medal. In the other heat, I had watched Viren and Puttemans soar away from the pack with their sub-4-minute-mile speed.

In the final, Dave Bedford of Great Britain took us out at a hard pace, and the race played out with the feel of a time trial—it was a war of attrition. I maintained contact with the lead pack until late in the race. Finally, at the start of the bell lap, I got dropped. I ran as hard as I could; those other guys were simply faster. I finished fifth in 27:51, almost 13 seconds behind Viren, the gold medalist, but I had whittled my American-record time by another 7 seconds. I looked up at those numbers on the scoreboard and knew that no other marathoner could touch my track speed. More important, I knew that I could recover in plenty of time for the marathon. My 10-K performance reinforced my plan to put the marathon away with a surge at the 9-mile mark.

I calculated that a 4:30 surge would open a 30-second lead over the rest of the pack. I then estimated how fast the other athletes would have to run, how hard they'd have to work, to make up that margin. All I needed to do, by contrast, was maintain a comfortable pace; that is, comfortable for me. Basically, after my surge, all I had to do was not slow down. I knew I could do that because I'd be running at a pace significantly slower than what I had just run on the track in the 10.

The numbers looked promising, but I couldn't grow overconfident; I couldn't get hung up on the idea of "winning." I had already developed a theory concerning the competitive dynamic of a marathon. In any given world-class race, you had 10 runners who were capable of winning. But of those 10, only three were going to have a good day on marathon day. The goal was to be one of those three men blessed by the marathon gods. The 10-K had shown me I stood a good chance of being among the select.

I knew I was fit. I knew I was peaking at the right time. My overarching training strategy was based on sharpening my strengths rather than improving on my weaknesses; my strength was the ability to recover. Years later, exercise physiologists at the Cooper Clinic in Dallas would determine that I only had an average VO_2-max reading—the measure of how efficiently your body processes oxygen. However, my capacity for operating at my maximum level of oxygen assimilation was off the charts. In my post-surge miles, to maintain a solid pace and hold my lead, I could run at a level well below maximum effort.

In short, mentally, physically, and emotionally, I was ready for my marathon. History, however, was about to intervene.

12

Black September

On the evening of September 4, I crashed as usual on the floor of the balcony and fell asleep at once. Early on the morning of the 5th, when it was still dark, I was awakened by a single loud crack that sounded like gunfire. The sound didn't repeat, however, so I rolled over and went back to sleep. I felt secure in my rest and intent on my goal. What danger could possibly touch me here, deep in the heart of the Olympic Village? Of course, looking back, who could have imagined that, years earlier, violence could have visited the doctor's children in their beds in the big fine house on Highland Avenue?

I would soon learn the truth: In the predawn hours, eight Palestinian terrorists, wearing sweat suits so that they appeared like athletes staggering back to their quarters after a late night on the town, had scaled the chain-link fence at the rear of the village. They pounded on the door of the suite housing a number of Israeli athletes. One of the Israelis, wrestling referee Yosef Gutfreund, realized what was happening and blocked the doorway from inside. The terrorists shot and killed him and broke through the door, seizing 11 hostages.

That was the shot that woke me on my balcony, about 100 meters across the courtyard. But it had been just one shot, and I had gone back to sleep. I awakened again in the gray light of dawn and knew at once that things were amiss. The courtyard below was still and silent. Even at this early hour the place should have been bustling. I had learned to sleep through the normal clamor of a village morning and even found the noises to be comforting. Now, there was only silence. Something was off; something was wrong.

I rose from the floor and looked down at the courtyard: empty. I went inside the apartment, where my roommates and a few other American athletes, including Pre, were huddled around the unit's tiny black-and-white TV set. It was tuned to a news bulletin from a local station; this was long before the advent of CNN and other cable news outlets. Pre's mother was German-American, and Steve had grown up speaking the language. He translated for us, relaying the news that, at first, seemed too shocking to believe.

For a long while we stayed glued to the TV and to Pre's staccato, translated narration, until the reality had sunk in. Then we turned to each other, not knowing what to do. No word came from law enforcement authorities, no instructions issued from our Olympic Committee. So we deferred to the default instinct of young men and went to the dining hall to eat breakfast.

The cafeteria was open, the steam trays brimming with food, athletes eating as usual—was this all a bad dream? Back to the apartment, back to the eerie silence of the courtyard, back to the tiny black-and-white TV. The age of televised urban terrorism had begun, less than 100 meters from where we were sitting. A fuzzy image of our apartment complex flitted across the screen. We broke away from the TV, moved out to the balcony to take a look. Nobody warned us that it was dangerous; there was no call for evacuation, no black-ops or SWAT team shoving us off the balcony to take up a sniper's position. We heard a knock on the door, but it wasn't an official. It was a kid named Hailu Ebba, a 1500-meter runner representing Ethiopia who had gone to Oregon State. He had come to our apartment seeking information and comfort from other Oregon guys.

For the next few hours we moved back and forth between the TV and the balcony, in a haze of adrenaline, anxiety, boredom, and disbelief. Finally the adrenaline and boredom took over, and our need for routine and some semblance of order kicked in. We were runners; we needed to go run. We had to train. Theoretically the village was in lockdown, but it was easy to get around that. We put on our gear and proceeded to the back gate of the village, which we always used to go to our workouts. The same security guys as always were there, but now they were scared, and now they held rifles. The guards told us we couldn't leave, but they were too freaked and confused to pay us much attention. So we eased away from the gate and, just as the Black September killers had done a few hours earlier, climbed the chain-link fence without difficulty.

We just ran easy. By now we knew that people were dead, that more would likely die, and that everything had changed. The rest of the Games would surely be cancelled. But that hardly mattered at that point. I remember running as if by automatic pilot, simultaneously noticing everything, especially that deep, radical silence that almost seemed solid, and noticing nothing, as if my head were filled with blocks of air.

We finished our run and returned to the apartment. Still no alert, still no evacuation order, still no information other than what we gleaned from the TV and Pre's translations. The screen showed a glimpse of one of the killers, a guy whose head was covered in a balaclava. We moved out to the balcony and looked across the courtyard, and there was the same guy as on TV—the balaclava, the Uzi—looking back at us from the balcony of the hostage apartment. The guy could have popped us. He could have raked us all with automatic rifle fire, as carelessly as my grandfather had raked his hand across the faces of his terrified children when the teddy bear flew out the car window on that day long ago. But today the killer just looked at us for a moment and then went back inside the apartment.

The silence from above continued. Nobody came to tell us anything. We just watched TV and tried to piece together what might be happening. The phone lines to the outside were jammed; we couldn't contact our significant others. It seemed frustrating at the time, but looking back I think relying totally on one another helped us think through events more effectively than if we'd been given instructions every step of the way. This was new for everybody. We were all sort of making it up as we went along.

That afternoon we went out for another run. By this time we assumed our Olympics—the Games we'd sweated for years—were finished, and that soon we'd be on a plane back to the States. We were no longer training; we were just using running to process events. Back at the village, Bowerman called a meeting of the track team and told us what he knew, which wasn't much more than we were getting. Later in the afternoon we heard a clatter overhead. We rushed out to the balcony to see a helicopter approaching: the chopper sent to pick up the terrorists and hostages and carry them to the airport. A few minutes later, the helicopter again, presumably carrying the killers and their hostages. Now an even deeper silence descended over the courtyard.

"Well, I guess we're kind of done," somebody said.

But somehow I knew it wasn't really over. We went to bed that night in the literal and figurative dark—still no word from any officials, and we remained cut off from people outside the village.

The next morning, the TV told us the terrible ending to the drama: Out at the airport, security forces had stormed the airplane holding the terrorists and their hostages. Eleven Israeli athletes died in the firefight, along with eight members of the Black September terrorist group.

The rest of that day passed in a blur. There was no media presence, no reporters climbing the fence to interview us, and there were no smartphones on which to text our people and let them know that we were okay. It was weird, as if it all were happening in another century, on another continent. We assumed the whole world was watching, and that back in the States our friends and families knew we were safe—indeed we were certain that they knew more about what had happened than we did, 100 meters away from the scene of the crime, the spot where a new dark age was born.

The next day we learned that, contrary to our expectations, the Games were going to continue. There was too much invested, too much at stake, and already, in the wake of the first attack of this kind, people realized that carrying on and living well formed the best revenge against terror. There would be a one-day pause to mourn the victims, with a memorial service to be held at the Olympic Stadium. The marathon, originally scheduled for September 9, would now take place on September 10. As soon as I got the word, my mind clicked back into focus. I resumed executing my detailed, painstakingly arranged plan. I knew in my bones that, collectively and individually, this was the proper response. Running my marathon was the best thing I could do.

My fellow marathoners felt the same way, although the catastrophe had altered their approach. Kenny Moore, for instance, told me after the memorial service that he'd be running in memory of the fallen hostages. I replied that I'd be doing the opposite; I would not give the terrorists a thought. Unconsciously, perhaps, I was echoing the behavior of my childhood. Dr. Sam had wanted to stomp around inside my head, dominate my every moment, and I responded by denying him that power, putting the man out of my mind.

The next day in the dining hall, Ron Hill, the British marathoncr who'd logged the fastest time in the world that year, brought his tray over during lunchtime. He sat down and started to complain. It was a totally terrible decision to delay the marathon, he said. "Don't they realize how carefully we have to prepare for this marathon and that changing the day screws up our schedule? How could they do this to us?"

"Ron, we've been training our whole lives for this race," I said. "One day isn't going to make a difference."

Ron kept muttering and sputtering, throwing himself off of his game more than the organizers had done by delaying the race. Ron Hill was definitely one of the 10 athletes who had a shot of winning the marathon. However, I now realized that he was unlikely to be one of the three runners who, according to my theory, would show their best on September 10.

Looking back at that terrible, surreal spate of time—the five days from the moment I heard the shot on my balcony to the moment the starting pistol cracked for my marathon—I recognized that my friends and I had been forced to go through all the stages of grief in a condensed, pressure-filled time frame: shock, denial, depression, anger, acceptance, resolve. We had no choice. There was no one guiding or protecting us, no one to rely on but one another.

13

The Invisible Thread

At 3 p.m. on September 10, 1972, I stepped to the starting line of the Munich Olympic Marathon. I felt the calmness that comes when you know that you've done everything within your power to prepare for a test. I also felt the thrill of anticipation that comes in the moment before a test, when you sense that everything is breaking your way. Everything, that is, except for the fact that, a few days earlier, I had listened to a fellow Olympian get murdered; the fact that 10 more of the victim's teammates had been slaughtered; the fact that a new age of terrorism had begun right under my nose; and the fact that a follow-up attack out on the wide-open marathon course was a distinct possibility.

But all of those facts, and all their implications, were out of my control, so I let them go. My provisional reaction to the massacre was to ride it out. It's going to unfold according to its own pace and rhythm, so wait to see what happens. I had a lot of experience in this kind of situation. Dealing with Dr. Sam had taught me the art of vigilance. By necessity, I had learned to read a room—to anticipate how people were going to act and react and to locate the exits and lanes of escape. Maybe I was just a little more at home in chaos than my brother marathoners.

I regarded the race itself with a similar sort of engaged detachment. I was about to find out if my surge-and-recovery tactic was going to work. As much as I'd invested in my plan—all of my body, mind, and heart—I could take a step back from it, treading a cool mental edge. Just wait for the gun to go off. Feed off the buzz, but don't take too big a bite. Draw just the proper measure of energy from the crowd. This was the Olympic Games, but it was also only a track meet. Here I am. Take it step by step and see what happens.

The gun, the leap from the line, the break to the inside lane, the parading out of the stadium and into the city, the falling in with the leaders at a 5-minute-a-mile pace that, for an Olympic marathoner, feels comfortably within one's lactate threshold. Five miles, 8 miles, here comes the Nymphenburg Castle, and oh yes, oh man, this still feels good. Here it comes . . . the fountain, the 150-degree bend, and bam! A mile-long bull rush that blew open a 1,000-meter lead.

It still felt good. It still felt way short of maximum effort. I had built a reputation as a heady, cerebral sort of competitor, but the truth was I raced on feel—how I was feeling, how the other runners must be feeling when they watched me blast away, how they would feel a few miles down the road when they'd contemplate the energy expenditure it would take to reel me back in. I felt my own energy pulsing inside, almost separate from me; in the parlance of *The Teachings of Don Juan,* a best-selling book of the era, I felt my *nagual.* I was almost playing with it—how long to dole out the effort, when to dial it back, how close I could get to the edge without tipping over the line. It wasn't something I thought about; it was a way of knowing that those hundreds upon hundreds of intervals—those 35-second 200s, those 20 × 800s— had drilled into my bones.

Once I was cleanly out front and running alone, I started to think again, plotting when I could throttle back from my surge. Because I knew the course so well, because I'd trained over almost every mile, learning the angle of the turns and the slant of the sunlight and the texture of the road surface beneath the tissue-thin soles of my racing flats, I was able to conceive of the distance in segments. I didn't think about running 17 more miles; I just thought about running each 5-K stretch between time clocks, moving from segment to segment to segment. The Nymphenburg Palace to the English Garden. The English Garden to the Pinakothek art museum, the Pinakothek to Sendlinger Tor. It was the same way I thought when I raced the 10,000; you go lap by lap, mile-split by mile-split. I was carrying out my plan to approach the marathon as if it were only a very long track race.

Meanwhile, behind me, the other runners still appeared to be thinking like traditional, steady-state, war-of-attrition marathoners. On the track, when a runner threw a midrace surge, the rest of the lead pack went with him, or at least kept him in their sights and within striking distance. When I made my mile-9 surge in Munich, however, those other guys let me escape. Given the course's frequent bends and turns, I was immediately out of sight. This was a considerable psychological advantage. In any kind of distance race, there's an invisible thread that stretches about 10 meters. If a competitor is running 10 meters or less in front of you, you don't worry about him; you know you can pull even or spurt past him just about any time you choose. But once a guy hammers a gap of more than 10 meters, then you start to worry. Then you start calculating the hurt and juice it will take to close the gap. Soon you start to worry that you won't be able to close it at all.

Not only had I snapped that invisible 10-meter thread, I had disappeared entirely.

Now I was running alone. It was just me and the long blue line that traced the 26.2-mile route through Old Munich, the city where I had been born. I was only vaguely aware of the crowds lining the course. In those days there were no barriers separating the sidewalk from the road, and not even the terrorist attack had induced the authorities to beef up security out on the marathon course. Not that it would have done much good anyway. Today, in the 21st century, marathons are run in cities everywhere around the world, including the capitals of the most repressive regimes, but I think that the marathon expresses the essence of the free, open, democratic, cosmopolitan spirit. As the 2013 Boston Marathon bombing so tragically proved, a marathon course is vulnerable by its very nature. In 1972, in Munich, at the dawn of the age of urban terrorism—and the dawn of the age of the modern running movement—the marathon was at its most vulnerable.

Before the race, Kenny, Jack, and I had briefly speculated that a follow-up attack was possible. We were all potential targets, but now, running alone out in front, with the ABC cameras following my every step, with my drooping mustache and the letters USA emblazoned across my singlet (in 1972, the dispiriting end of the Vietnam War era, America's global standing was at its nadir), I might as well have had a bull's-eye painted on my back. Had I not been so absorbed in my race—in following my plan, traveling from segment to segment, calibrating my effort, riding my pain—I might have been unnerved. As it was, true to my pledge to Kenny, I did not give the massacre a thought. My boyhood had taught me to avoid the what-ifs. And if an attack had materialized, my boyhood had also taught me how to escape. Whatever was going to happen was going to happen.

In the English Garden, around the 21-mile mark, I came to a bridge and saw my friend Roy Benson, a runner I knew from

Gainesville who would later become a prominent coach and exercise physiologist. As I crossed the bridge, Roy cupped his hands to his mouth and shouted that I had a 90-second lead—spectators along the course would often call out these sorts of updates, but Roy was a source I could trust. That news set the wheels turning in my head. A 90-second margin translated to more than a quarter mile. In order to close that gap, I would either have to slow down precipitously, my pursuer or pursuers would have to throw a surge equal to the one I had executed at the 9-mile mark, or a combination of those two things would have to happen.

Neither seemed likely. I was clicking along comfortably at a 5-minute-mile pace; or, more precisely, I was riding my pain, managing the bone-deep, full-body toothache that comes from running that fast for that long, no matter how good a shape you're in. At any rate, I wasn't going to slow down, and I knew from their past performances that none of the other contenders—not Kenny or Hill or Wolde or Clayton—was capable of mounting that quality of surge at that point in the race. In short, barring a disaster, no one was going to catch me.

Now there was only a mile to go. I ran down a wide boulevard called the Leopoldstrasse. The Olympic Stadium lifted into view, built over a crater dug by American bombs during the Second World War, its vaulting, acrylic-glass canopies embodying themes of peace, hope, and rebirth—a wistful thought in the wake of the massacre. From across the narrowing distance I could hear the surflike roil of the crowd.

I would cross the finish line within minutes. Rather than feeling jubilant, I felt quietly, almost grimly, satisfied. Apparently, I had gotten this one right. Now I recalled one of the cardinal tenets of the sport, a lesson I had learned back at Mount Hermon Academy from George Bowman: Work through the finish. Never take victory for granted. Just as I was about to enter the tunnel leading into the stadium, I heard a roar from the crowd. It was the final day of track-and-field competition but not the final day of the Games; I assumed an athlete had just cleared a major height in the high jump or pole vault.

And now my moment was nigh, the air-guitar fantasy moment that every runner dreams about: gliding out of the shadowed tunnel and into the light and roar of the Olympic Stadium, 60,000 spectators and a worldwide TV audience welcoming my triumphant arrival. For a moment I was Pheiddipides, finishing my run from the battlefield at Marathon, announcing with my dying breath that the Persians were defeated. This was my moment, and I opened myself for the roar, but instead my entry into the stadium was greeted by silence.

What's going on? I wondered. I know I'm an American. I know that nobody likes us nowadays, but give me a break . . . then I heard an American voice drift down from the stands: "Don't worry, Frank! You've got it!"

This was strange. Why should I worry? Of course I had gotten it; my closest pursuer was still out on the course, at least 90 seconds back.

Now I noticed a commotion at the finish line, and the strange silence of the crowd had given way to a piercing collective whistle, the European manner of booing. Only later would I learn what had happened. One more pulse of weirdness had hit the Munich Games. An imposter had run into the stadium 38 seconds before me: a young man wearing the facsimile of the all-white uniform of the West German track team. The interloper duped the waiting crowd into thinking one of their countrymen had magically appeared to win the gold medal.

Up in the ABC broadcast booth, Erich Segal, my former classics professor at Yale and a pioneering citizen-runner hired by the network to provide "expert" commentary, recognized the stunt right away. Amid the tumult, Erich seemed to forget that millions of people were listening to him back in the States. "He's a fake!" the professor shouted. "Get that guy off the track! Get him off now! You're the real winner, Frank!"

A beat later, the crowd realized what was happening. That was the instant when I ran into the stadium. Amid the very Greek-like pandemonium, I might have been the calmest person in the arena.

Finally, over the last 200 meters, the silence turned into cheers, and I had my truncated, belated moment. I crossed the line in 2:12:19.8, the first American to win the Olympic Marathon since Johnny Hayes at the 1908 London Games. Later, some historians would say that that moment gave birth to the modern running boom. But only one thought kept running through my brain: My plan had worked; I had gotten this one right.

✦ ✦ ✦

I looked up at the scoreboard and registered my time. I laced my fingers together at the back of my head and gave a smile. Then I walked back to the line to wait for the other guys to cross—my habit at every race I entered. About 2 minutes later, although it seemed longer, Karel Lismont of Belgium ran in to claim the silver medal. Who would be next? I hoped to see Kenny, but Mamo Wolde won the bronze. And in fourth place, only 80 yards behind Wolde, came my friend, mentor, and training partner, Kenny Moore. Kenny had run gallantly, giving his all, but not quite well enough for a medal.

"How did you do?" he asked me after he crossed.

"I won it," I said.

Kenny nodded. By the standard operating procedure for today's Olympics, the media ritual would have started right there and then. A network "correspondent" would have stuck a microphone into my face and asked what I was thinking when I launched my surge or when I ran into the stadium. Next, some countryman would have handed me a full-size American flag, which I would have jubilantly waved as I trotted around the track on my victory lap, grinning under the avalanche of smartphone snapshots. Then would come the show of drug testing, followed by the medal ceremony, during which a network camera would have panned in for a tight shot, showing my eyes glittering and my lips trembling as I sang along with the "The Star-Spangled Banner."

But none of that happened at Munich in 1972. Just as there had been no TV hype before the marathon—no soft-focus lifestyle profile describing my years of effort and sacrifice, etc.—there were no reporters or cameramen chasing me around the track immediately after the race. It never occurred to me to take a victory lap. Even if we weren't still mourning the slain Israeli athletes, even if all the flags in the stadium hadn't been flying at half-staff, I wouldn't have considered such an act. Victory laps, ostentatious shows of triumph, weren't my style. With the exception of outliers such as Muhammad Ali, Joe Namath, and Reggie Jackson, they were not the style for any athlete of that era.

By the same token, had someone handed me an American flag, I'm sure I would have respectfully draped it over my shoulders. I was proud and grateful to be an American; you just didn't wear patriotism on your sleeve in 1972. America was recalibrating its place in the world. The swagger we had earned starting back in 1945, right here in Germany, when we led the Allies to victory in World War II, had been hobbled by the Vietnam conflict and by the injustices dramatically protested on the Olympic stage four years earlier, when the American sprinters Tommie Smith and John Carlos electrified the world with their Black Power salute on the medal podium at the Mexico City Games. Finally, in 1972, despite the Munich Massacre, the surrogate cold war combat, and encroaching corporate commercialism, a vestige of the classical Olympic spirit prevailed—the idea that, for the brief span of an Olympiad, the flames of nationalism should be banked rather than fanned.

So no, I did not grin for the TV cameras, I did not take a victory lap, and I did not wrap myself in Old Glory. I shook hands with my competitors, my partners in this exacting, absorbing enterprise, accepting their congratulations and congratulating them in turn. Then I attended to some housekeeping. For a little extra cushioning during a marathon, I would tape support pads in my racing flats. By marathon's end I invariably suffered a blister where the insert rubbed against my skin. So it was today in Munich. I sat down trackside, took off my shoes, and started to doctor my bare and bleeding feet. An official approached and quietly asked me to take care of that inside the locker room, please.

A short time later, during the medal ceremony, I did feel a quiet but fierce throb of patriotic emotion. During a time of dissent and self-doubt, I had achieved something that my country could be proud of. An American hadn't won a gold medal in the marathon for more than 60 years. Since 1960 the gold medalists had come from Ethiopia—Abebe Bikila and Mamo Wolde. I had ended our dry spell. I had proved that an American could prevail in the longest and most difficult Olympic track-and-field event.

Standing on the podium, I also felt a jolt of personal pride. Again, not because I had won, or not solely because I had won. I felt proud because the marathon was pitiless, because it ruthlessly exposed your weaknesses and made you pay for every mistake. To succeed in the marathon, again in the parlance of *The Teachings of Don Juan,* a runner had to be impeccable. Today, for two hours and 10 minutes on the streets of Munich, Germany, to the utmost of my ability, I had been impeccable.

Fate had done its part—all of the breaks had fallen my way. I had met my goal, which wasn't to win, but to have the best day possible and finish in the top three. In and of itself, winning didn't drive me, nor did it drive guys like Kenny and Pre. It may sound corny, trite, self-evident, whatever, but it's the truth: We wanted to get the best out of ourselves. The gold medal, in the end, was no more than the wonderful by-product of the training I had put into my marathon.

Did my life change when I stepped down from the podium? Did a squadron of PR guys wait to stuff me into a limo and take me to a champagne reception where I would take a call from the White House? Not hardly. I went into the holding room and gathered my gear. It had started to rain, the adrenaline had worn off, and I was sore and tired, so I caught the last bus of the day back to the athletes' village. The bus door opened and there, amazingly, was Bob Giegengack, who was attending the Games as a liaison for the US Olympic Committee.

The last time I'd see Gieg had been a month earlier, in Oslo, when he'd timed me during an interval session: 4×800 meters at about 2 minutes per rep; what amounted to two miles of running at a sub-4-minute-mile pace. "Frankie," he had said, "you're ready."

Now, on the bus after the marathon, I greeted my old coach as if we were resuming our conversation on training. I told him all about the race, my thinking and my tactics, how I'd prepared. I knew if anybody could understand and appreciate the story, that person would be Gieg.

My old coach nodded. "Frankie," he said, "you had a great race." In his Brooklyn Elmer Fudd voice, it sounded like "gwate ways."

I told Gieg I owed a lot to him. He had taught me to trust myself; more specifically, he had taught me the physiological and competitive benefits of hard interval training. "Frankie," he said, "you've been coaching yourself since the middle of your junior year."

I got off the bus, and that night I went out to dinner with Louise's family, Nanette, Erich Segal, and a few other friends. The mood was celebratory but, given the weight of events, not quite exultant. I will say this: On the night after a marathon, you have the capacity to put away a lot of beer. The beer that night in Munich was the best I had ever tasted.

14

Letting the Beast Out

The next day, Kenny and I went for a very brief recovery jog in the Olympic park outside the village. We located a sauna and sat down and baked out the hurt and rehashed the race. After his disappointing fourth-place finish, he had to do some reframing. He explained he had been running beside Mamo Wolde, about a minute behind me. Around the 20-mile mark, Wolde surged. Kenny tried to go with him, but his thigh cramped up. Then I told Kenny my story.

Despite the consuming effort, I recovered quickly. Recovery has always been my ace in the hole, my single defining physical gift. By most physiological measures, I am an average among the elites, but at the top when it comes to overall running efficiency and ability to recover from hard efforts. Two or three days out from the marathon, I was feeling pretty loose and hungry to start training again. By contrast, no one seemed eager to talk about the Munich Massacre. We were all a little stunned, and again, this was all new. Other than our instinctive gathering around the TV set as the catastrophe unfolded, we had not yet learned the ritual that has come to define contemporary acts of urban terrorism—the compulsive immersion in the sea of video replays and media analyses.

By the same token, I had no model for how a marathon gold medalist was supposed to act. I had no inkling of the opportunities or pitfalls awaiting me; the modern sports marketing juggernaut was then in its infancy. I never assumed I would fall back on the old Bob Richards Wheaties-box formula. Nor did I consider pursuing small-scale opportunities that wouldn't run afoul of the outdated but inescapable amateur rules. However, I did allow myself one fantasy. I imagined returning in triumph to Mount Hermon, addressing the boys at an assembly in the chapel and thanking Sam Green and Warren Hall. However, in terms of fame or celebrity, I did have one negative example, a figure on a path that I decided I was not going to take.

After winning seven gold medals in swimming, Mark Spitz, a Californian, was far and away the star of the Munich Games. A certain degree of hype preceded him into the competition, and after each of his victories—each time he delivered under increasingly intense pressure—the number of agents and handlers around Spitz grew. One day after the massacre, I stopped by the housing office of the village. Spitz and his team were in there, conferring anxiously on how to spirit the swimmer out of the city, out of harm's way. Meanwhile, the rest of us were going through the cafeteria line at the dining hall and getting ready for our events. Nothing against Mark Spitz: Due to his celebrity and the fact that he was the highest-profile Jewish athlete at the Munich Games, he was more of a target than the rest of us. By going with the marketers, moreover, he was only trying to leverage his moment, to finally cash in after years of busting his butt for no bucks whatsoever. Still, I decided that if and when my moment came—if I happened to win the marathon and if the world took notice—I would handle myself differently.

On the charter flight from Munich to JFK Airport in New York City, we did not discuss the massacre—we didn't have the vocabulary—and I did not anticipate an appearance on *Good Morning America,* a TV show that did not yet exist (although the next year, in 1973, I did appear as a guest on *The Tonight Show* with Johnny Carson). Instead, a limo picked me up at the airport and took me to a celebration in Middletown.

A hometown welcome was in order after my gold medal performance, but there was some confusion about which was really my hometown. I had grown up in Middletown but had lived most of the time in Gainesville; I listed my parent's home in Taos as my official legal address. After the debacle with the attack on the hippie girl and the subsequent three-day shotgun feud, however—the episode had gone public and even earned a write-up in *Life* magazine—some people in New Mexico wanted to keep their distance from me. Meanwhile, outside of our tight little Florida Track Club (FTC) family, no one in Gainesville knew I was living there. I had grown up and started running in Middletown, so the town rightly claimed me as its own. Louis Mills, the county commissioner, sent the car down to JFK to pick up Louise and me and whisk us up the Hudson River Parkway to my hero's welcome.

I hadn't been in Middletown since the spring of 1969, when I stayed with Barbara, and she had timed my run at the high school track before I won my outdoor NCAA title in the 10,000. Nanette had moved away, so Louise and I lodged at my grandmother's house. The next morning I went out for a run along the same streets I had covered as a boy, and that evening we went to the hotel ballroom for the gala in my honor. Everything was going fine—I was greeting old friends such as the Prestons, I was laughing and exchanging hugs and shaking hands—until I turned, and there was my father. There was Dr. Sam.

Louis Mills hadn't told me about my father because he wanted it to be a surprise. I think Louis himself was somewhat surprised;

without telling anyone, continuing his style of throwing others off balance and calling attention to himself, instead of doing the logical thing and getting on an airplane (or doing the merciful thing and not coming at all), my father drove solo 2,000 miles across the country to attend my celebration (my mother, predictably, stayed in Taos). Now here he was, shaking just as many hands and fielding just as many hugs as I was. Many of the citizens were as glad to welcome home their former doctor as they were to greet me.

When I saw my father, I was so startled, so befuddled from all the excitement and attention, that when he came to hug me, I accepted his embrace. I threw my arms around his shoulders, and a photographer from the Middletown newspaper snapped a picture that appeared on the front page of the next day's edition (along with a quote from Louis Mills: "Dr. Sam is the greatest humanitarian I have ever known."). I would like to report that the photo completely distorted my feelings, that in fact I resented my father showing up at an event honoring my running, when he had never bothered to attend any of my races when I was a boy or younger man. You might think that I would recoil from the man who had secretly tortured me and my family, but that was not the case. My feelings were more complicated. Even after all his crimes, he was still my father; he still had power over me, I still feared him, and on some murky level I wanted to please him. Somewhere inside of me, I still craved my father's approval.

Only after an hour or so, after by first- and second-hand I had heard enough of his malarkey, did my emotions return to center. "I couldn't even watch Frank's marathon on TV because it made me too nervous," my father told his admirers. I knew that was baloney. He had never watched any of my races, the Olympics included. My siblings had tuned in to the telecast, however, and years later my sister Mary told me how Dr. Sam had tried to spoil the experience for them.

"You can bet Frank is going to get a big head now," she recalls my father saying. Instead of watching me receive my gold medal, Mary says, my father turned away from the TV and walked into the next room.

+ + +

In terms of glamour and celebration, that was all I needed. The town that had unwittingly helped me survive had expressed its thanks. I didn't need any more adulation; that wasn't why I had gone to the Olympics. I was only 24, about to turn 25, and felt as if I were just starting to figure out this running thing. I was eager to return to my routine, so simple in design but taxing in execution, which had delivered my gold medal.

In effect I had two jobs, both athlete and coach, and I found the roles equally absorbing. I was aware of the running movement building in the general population, and just weeks after Munich there was already speculation that my gold medal run might catalyze a boom, but I didn't pay that much attention. For my purposes, the American running community was still a tightly knit group of about half a dozen close friends and like-minded training partners living in and moving among Gainesville, Boulder, and Eugene. Those guys were my family, the tracks and trails formed my refuge, and my training served as my intellectual, physical, and emotional outlet. I just wanted to get back to all that as quickly as possible, continue getting it right, and see where that would take me next.

I was halfway through law school in Florida at this point and returned to my studies in the fall after taking a leave during the spring and summer semesters of 1972. That December I joined up with the FTC for the national cross-country championships in San Diego; we won the team title, and I won the individual crown.

Then I flew to Japan to successfully defend my Fukuoka Marathon title, recording my PR of 2:10:30.

At that race I led from the gun. At the halfway point I threw down a surge, widening my lead, and then settled back to a sustainable pace that I rode on to the finish. By now my competitors knew what was coming, but there wasn't much they could do about it.

After Fukuoka in December, I resumed work on my law degree back in Gainesville. I always felt stronger when I had an intellectual pursuit to balance my training, and I always wanted to finish any project I started. Also, amateurism still reigned, and the law profession formed my fallback position. How else was I going to earn a living? We moved into a house with John Parker and his wife, Vivian. I wanted to get right back into my normal routine and let the aftereffects of Munich settle.

Still, even from within my bubble, I was aware of building change, of tectonic plates shifting. Mostly it was bright and hopeful—it was that same energy, that same magic, we had sensed at the Olympic Trials in Eugene the year before. With the first manifestations of the 1960s aquarian movement—the drug culture, the peace movement, full-scale progressive political change—falling back to Earth like the booster rocket of a NASA spacecraft, a more inward, personal, spiritual dynamic was rising in its place. Distance running was emerging as part of that change: a thinking person's physical pursuit, as much a way of life as a sport, nonviolent, reliant on self-discipline and delivering self-transcendence, providing a path to improved health, untethered to the establishment, virgin territory requiring only a pair of shoes and a desire for entry.

At the same time, there was a darker, demonic force at play, the one personified by the Black September killers in Munich, by that terrorist in a balaclava staring at me across the courtyard of the Olympic Village, holding an Uzi. Never as clean as people imagined it to be, the Olympic movement had lost its last vestige of innocence. In contrast to the new and hopeful energy of the citizen's running movement, Olympic-level running had become the province of power, politics, lies, cynicism, and, increasingly, performance-enhancing drugs.

Entirely unwittingly, by an accident of timing and history, I had emerged as one of the leaders of this new movement. On ABC, millions of people watched me running my marathon in Munich and saw a new kind of sports hero—a skinny, long-haired kid with a mustache. People couldn't imagine slicing through the water like Mark Spitz or flying and spinning like the gymnast Olga Korbut, but almost anybody believed they could run like Frank Shorter.

I might have been one of the new lights, but my star paled in comparison to that of Steve Prefontaine's. Out in Eugene, Pre was catalyzing a totally organic, totally authentic flowering of the running culture. Along with steadily improving as a performer, continuing to follow the arc that had been rising since he arrived in Eugene from Coos Bay, Pre had grown more self-assured, deepening in maturity without losing any of the heart and fire that had originally galvanized his fans. Moreover, Pre was thoroughly a West Coast guy, and the West Coast was where, in the early 1970s, in all senses of the term, the music was coming from. People admired and emulated my achievement, but they loved Pre.

So in Gainesville I finished up law school and continued following the same basic plan I'd been using for years: I trained like a 5-K runner while, as a competitor, I placed the bulk of my chips in the marathon. We were starving artists in some ways—I never made enough income to file a 1040 until 1974, and then just barely—but we never suffered. We pretty much traveled wherever we needed, albeit never first-class, and usually thanks to a lot of improvising.

During the summers of 1973 and '74, for instance, Pre and I would go on a barnstorm tour of the European track circuit. The organizers of one of the major meets in Zurich or Stockholm or Berlin would pay for our travel, then once we'd run in that meet, we would hit the road. We cruised through Finland in a Saab 99 with the old two-cylinder put-put engine, running small-town meets every couple of days, sharing one-star hotel rooms, making a few hundred dollars under the table, which helped support us through the rest of the year. In those pre-professional days, that was how most Olympic-level track-and-field athletes made it. That is, athletes from the West. The Eastern Bloc athletes, meanwhile, were supported relatively lavishly by their state federations (although they paid a steep price, but that's getting a little ahead of the story).

We slept on floors of cheap hotels and drove the Finnish outback, but we hardly felt deprived. Living was cheap back in Gainesville. With the Montreal Olympic Marathon in '76 as my long-range goal, I competed in one marathon a year—Fukuoka—and raced on the track the rest of the season. The 10 was my strength, but I remained competitive in the 5000 and even the 3000. In 1974 I won a big 10,000 in Stockholm where I set an Olympic stadium record, and I won shorter races in both Bislett, Norway, and Zurich. In 1975, I set an American record in the 10,000 and was the second-ranked 10,000-meter runner in the world; I also ranked third among Americans in the 5000 meters.

I finished law school and returned to Colorado in the summer of 1974. Louise and I moved to Denver, where she pursued a master's degree in library science and I studied for the state bar exam. I passed the exam in February of 1975 and we moved back to Boulder, which has been my home ever since. I often ran with Joe

French and Bob Stone, Boulder attorneys, who hired me to work part-time in their law firm. Joe remains one of my closest friends. Boulder was ideal for my purposes, with plentiful high-altitude trails and excellent facilities at the University of Colorado, which officials let me use for free. Boulder was the only town in America lying above 5,000 feet that had a regulation indoor running track, meaning I wouldn't have to travel to lower elevations for speed workouts and interval sessions during the winter.

The year 1974 turned into 1975, and time started to bend toward Montreal. I continued to follow the program that led to my success in Munich. By my lights it was same time, same station, but the scene around me was shifting. The old guard was changing. John Parker, Jeff Galloway, Jack Bacheler, and Kenny Moore, all a few years my senior, had transitioned away from Olympic-level training and competition. They continued to run and to serve as the wisest and most dynamic voices in the increasingly popular sport, but they had moved on to the next stages of their lives. A new group of guys were coming up—Craig Virgin, Duncan Macdonald, and Don Kardong. Steve Prefontaine, Dick Buerkle, and I were the three holdovers, still hard in the hunt for Montreal.

Pre and I had only spent time together in fits and starts, but those periods tended to be intense, and we got to know each other well. As I mentioned earlier, we were different in almost every respect, from age to event to background to temperament, except one: our conviction to go about the sport in the right way, in the manner we had learned from coaches like Bowerman and Dellinger and Giegengack, and from fellow runners such as Kenny Moore, Jack Bacheler, and John Parker. Pre and I both trained very hard, but it was always toward a purpose; we never worked for work's sake or to try to impress anybody.

Pre and I liked to train together because we brought out the best in one another. We didn't feel shy about letting the beast out—during some of our interval sessions we hit a level of ferocity that was almost frightening—and the best part about it, or maybe the most unsettling part, was that we didn't need to talk about it. Just a nod from Pre let me know it was time for me to step to the lead for an 800, and I could just shake my head to communicate no, we're not quite done yet, one more repeat.

When we weren't working, Pre felt okay about showing his quieter, more thoughtful side around me. By this time, 1975, his persona and legend were full-blown. In the popular imagination, Steve Prefontaine was this fiery, swashbuckling, balls-to-the-wall master of a sport that had been around forever but now was suddenly fashionable, a guy who always led with his heart and ran from the front, a rebel who went his own way and could party as hard as he trained. The man that I knew and worked beside was different, or more accurately, was more multi-dimensional.

Pre recognized that the sport was evolving out of an awkward and untenable amateurism. If American track-and-field athletes were going to compete with the state-sponsored athletes from the Eastern Bloc, then we had to become full-time professionals making a fair, aboveboard living. The change wasn't going to come from the calcified top levels of the sport, so we, the athletes, would have to push for reform. Pre took his leadership role in this movement quite seriously, almost as seriously as he took his training and racing, which, of course, formed the heart of our relationship.

15

What If

I might have been in the best shape of my life in the spring of 1975. The previous December I had finished second in the national cross-country championships and then traveled on to Japan, where I won my fourth consecutive Fukuoka title. In 1974, I was rated number one in the world at that distance. My legacy clearly lay with the marathon, but I prided myself on being a complete distance runner who was capable of running a top-shelf race at a range of events at almost any time of year. As I've explained, the thought and effort I put into my work at the shorter distances led directly to my success in the marathon. Steve Prefontaine admired my approach and wanted to learn more about it. That led to our training together in Colorado and then in Taos, New Mexico, in April 1975.

By this time Pre had graduated from the University of Oregon but had stayed in Eugene to work with Bill Dellinger. He had bought a share in a sports bar but was looking for something more solid—a career as a professional athlete. In Boulder, I was working a few hours a day for French & Stone, a local law firm. Steadily living and training at Boulder's 6,000-foot altitude provided a solid baseline, and at selected times during the year, I would travel to New Mexico to train for a week or so at the Taos Ski Valley, at near 9,000 feet. That April Pre asked if he could join me for a New Mexico stint.

Pre and his girlfriend joined Louise and me for a week in a Taos condo. The ski season was winding down, but the lifts were still open and the mountain featured excellent spring ski conditions. Pre wasn't a skier, but he took lessons and by the end of the week he could do just fine on the bunny and intermediate runs. Our routine: Ski from 9 a.m. to 11 a.m. At 11 we would put on our shoes and run 4 miles up the mountain, from 7,000 feet to 9,000 feet, and then 4 miles back down. In the afternoon we would ski again and run the mountain again: 15 miles a day total. We were up too high to run very fast, so it gave us plenty of time to talk. Pre told me about his ideas for developing a professional framework for the sport. He was planning on challenging the Amateur Athletic Union (AAU) by putting on a top-level track meet at Hayward Field in Eugene that wasn't sanctioned by the governing body.

Other times, other days, we were hurting too much for deep conversation. One day we ran downhill in freezing temperatures with the wind driving dagger points of snow into our exposed faces, searing our lungs, and Steve was pissing and moaning. He never shirked from the work, but he could bitch with the best of them. I told him, "Steve, no other runner in the world is working as hard or suffering as much as you and I are right now." He stopped complaining after that.

In the evenings the four of us would hang out at the St. Bernard Lounge with its owner, Jean Mayer, who was also one of the best skiers on the mountain. Jean and his brother Dadou were the two main engines of the local night life. It was true that Pre liked to party—we all did in those days—but not nearly as much as he was purported to, and we adhered to an ironclad rule: We never indulged to the point that it would detract in any way from our training the next morning. After running and skiing in the cold at 9,000- to 10,000-foot altitude all day, those jukebox nights ended early. That week seemed unexceptional at the time, more days at the office, but looking back now it seems golden.

About a month later—I recall it was a Tuesday, because Tuesday was a hard day on my schedule, and I had just finished a draining interval session on the track at the University of Colorado—my phone rang: It was Pre. Did I want to come out to Eugene and race the 5000 against him at a meet at Hayward on Friday?

"You know I went hard today," I said. "You just want somebody you can beat." Pre laughed. He said he'd pay for my plane ticket and that I could stay with Kenny Moore and Bobbie at their house.

And then he explained the deal. The meet was the consequence of the talks we'd had in Taos in April. Pre was one of the principal organizers of a track meet that would challenge the AAU hegemony over the sport. Without AAU sanction, Pre had invited the Finnish national team, then on tour in the United States, to compete in a special track meet at Hayward Field. Also afoul of AAU regulations, Pre was openly paying all expenses—what amounted to an appearance fee—for the Finns. The key to the meet, and the key to the challenge, was a match race in the 5000 between Pre and Lasse Viren, the Finnish runner who'd won the gold at the event at the Munich Games. By the letter of their law, the AAU could penalize all who participated in the meet, even stripping athletes of "amateur" status, which would prevent them from competing in all the important events around the world. The stakes were high: If the AAU allowed the meet, their whole house of cards would crumble; the athletes, meanwhile, were risking their careers. But the meet organizers in Eugene were betting that the governing body would never disqualify Pre and Viren, who, worldwide, were the two most popular runners in the sport.

That was the setting; those were the stakes. The Finns were on board; the Eugene running community, including Bowerman and the fledgling shoe company, Nike, stood behind the event; and all the seats would be filled in the Hayward grandstands. Now, at the last minute, a potential calamity: Viren was sick, had scratched, and Pre wanted me to step in for the Finn.

I agreed at once. The cause was just, the action was well thought out, and I wasn't about to let down a friend. I sensed that the timing was right for this sort of move. Back in college I had shied away from the marches and demonstrations and boycotts, convinced that, at that stage, my job was to listen rather than speak out, build my power and wait for the right time to act, when I had enough knowledge and influence to really make a difference. Well, I had accrued some power, and the time for change was now.

The meet was scheduled for Friday, May 25, just before the Memorial Day weekend. I flew out to Eugene on Thursday. Kenny picked me up and took me to the cottage that he and his wife, Bobbie, had bought near Hendricks Park in the hills above the campus of the University of Oregon.

I found the atmosphere around Eugene to be similar to that during the '72 Olympic Trials, only more so—more electricity, more enthusiasm, more of the sense that this town formed the epicenter of a powerful new movement. America had recently endured the debacle of Watergate and the humiliating end to the Vietnam War. The nation was looking for any avenue to renewal. Eugene was brimming with this fresh energy—students and citizens out hammering the trails along the Willamette and packing the Hayward stands to cheer on the Sundance Kid who personified the new passion, the new hope: Steve Prefontaine.

There was a special energy to this track meet, which Pre had organized as a blow against the established powers in track and field—and, by extension, against the corrupt and ineffectual old order in general. Pre put up world-class times in distances ranging from the mile to the 10,000, but the 5000—a race of roughly 3 miles—was his wheelhouse event, and fans were already anticipating a rematch between Pre and Viren at the 1976 Olympics in Montreal. I couldn't match Viren's speed in the 5, but I could come close, and among American track and running fans I was a name known second only to Pre.

In fact, the year before, Pre and I had engaged in a 3-mile match race right here at Hayward. He and I had traded the lead all during the race, almost as if we were knocking out training intervals. The wind was so strong that we would cover each half-lap two seconds slower than the half-lap we ran with the wind at our backs. We had stayed together until the final two laps, when it became every man for himself. Pre had out-leaned me at the tape, running an American record 12:51.8, while I finished in 12:51.9. The Hayward crowd went bananas.

The fans were hoping for a show of similar caliber during this meet, but that was unlikely, due to the draining interval session I'd logged just days earlier. Still, I gave the race my all, hanging with Pre until about 600 meters out, when he pulled away to win in 13:23. I followed in second place about seven seconds later. My time and place didn't matter. What mattered was that Pre and I had shown up. We knew we had justice and common sense on our side. We were young and in our prime, with a seemingly unlimited supply of tomorrows at our disposal. Pre was already talking about joining me in Taos next spring for another week of skiing and running. We had made it through the Munich Massacre together. We were on the right side of the times, of history, and what did we have to fear from the AAU?

The sun was shining, and the girls were smiling. Before our

race, which was the final one of the day's schedule, Pre and I stretched out on the infield grass to watch the action and just sort of hang out. A photographer snapped a picture—Pre with a shock of hair falling over his eye, chewing on a blade of grass—and I'm sitting right beside him, squinting in the sunlight.

After the meet I jogged back to Kenny's cottage, and that evening we all went to Geoff Hollister's house for a party—Geoff was a good friend of Kenny's and Pre's and one of Nike's first employees. We stayed for a while; everybody was certainly having a good time, but it wasn't a raucous let-it-rip kind of scene. It was the kind of gathering where people had a lot of important things to discuss. There was a heady, almost conspiratorial air—the sense we were breaking new ground, approaching fresh territory.

Somewhere in there Kenny and Bobbie went home, but I decided to stay a while longer. There were plenty of friends around who could drop me back at Kenny's place. In the movie version of Pre's life, the film *Without Limits,* my character develops a toothache from recent wisdom teeth extraction and asks the Prefontaine character to give him a ride home. The filmmaker, Robert Towne, took some artistic license. I did not have a toothache, but I did catch a ride back to Kenny's cottage with Pre.

Pre wasn't drunk. There was no way I would have gotten in the car with him—I wouldn't have let him get behind the wheel—if he'd been loaded. I had been with him at a lot of parties and bars, and I knew the signs of drunkenness. We were also mindful of our unspoken but clearly understood rule—to never go past the point where we'd feel impaired for the next morning's work. Pre and I had already made a plan to meet the next morning for a 10-mile tempo run.

I climbed down into Pre's MGB sports car, and he zipped me a short distance through the hilly neighborhood to Kenny and

Bobbie's cottage. Along the way we talked about the day and its implications, projecting the likely responses from the AAU officials and how we might respond in turn. We realized we had only taken a baby step toward true professional status, but that first step was vital. We discussed how this might impact the fledgling road racing scene in the United States. Road races of 10-K and other distances were starting to pop up in cities across America, and many invited elite-level runners to compete. At the very least, Pre and I agreed, we should have our expenses paid without worrying about AAU sanctions and penalties. After all, appearance fees were common and travel expenses were legal.

Pre pulled up in front of Kenny's house. He cut the engine, and we continued talking for a few minutes. He was lucid and engaged and sure he was doing the right thing for his fellow athletes and himself. Pre would have preferred not to hassle with all these issues—he would much rather have poured everything into training and racing—but this fight had chosen him. Now that he was in it, Pre appeared to relish the battle. After confirming our time to go running in the morning, I climbed out of the car. Pre started the engine and pulled away, and I listened to the receding whine of the motor as he rounded the corner out of sight, headed home. I noticed that he took the shorter, steeper route down the butte. There were a series of blind turns on that road, virtual switchbacks, and for safety we avoided running that road.

I let myself into Kenny's house and crashed out in bed. Very early the next morning, Kenny shook my shoulder. "Steve's dead," he told me.

I bolted out of bed, and Kenny told me as much as he knew: a single-car crash, up at a bend in the road, perhaps half a mile away. The accident had happened just moments after Pre had dropped me off.

In the first gray light of dawn, Kenny and I walked uphill to the scene of the crash. At that moment you're focused on the details, on the hows and whens, on the angles and the patterns, almost as if you're reliving that moment and with a slight adjustment you can prevent the accident from occurring. Your friend isn't dead, that couldn't be possible, you're meeting him in a half hour to take a 10-mile run. We looked at the still-fresh skid marks, the detritus of broken glass under the flat slab of rock face, sheer as a retaining wall, where the MGB had augered in, bounced away, and flipped over upside down, trapping Pre underneath the car body and crushing out his life in a moment.

Kenny and I walked back to his place, sat there stunned, fielding phone calls, reliving the last few hours, piecing the story together. We were in shock. It was like the moment three years before in Munich, only magnified a hundred times. An act even more random, more radically out of tune with the tenor of the day. Death coming in the pulsing heart of life. Steve Prefontaine was too alive to be dead. He and I had just been talking about what was going to happen next. We had been talking about it right in front of the house a few hours earlier. We had been so absorbed in the conversation that Pre had cut the engine, and we sat there for a few minutes, talking it out. What if he had just dropped me off without stopping to talk? What if our conversation had lasted five seconds more or five seconds less? What if I had stayed at the party another half hour? Wouldn't that have let Steve off the hook, caused him to miss his appointment with the wall . . . wouldn't Pre and I be hammering our miles right at this moment?

And just like Munich, not knowing what else to do, Kenny and I went out for a run that afternoon. We ran down to the river to let things settle out. Crossing the footbridge over the Willamette near

Autzen Stadium, I expected to see Pre running toward me. The accident was all anybody could talk about, but no matter how many times we went over it, it didn't add up. Pre had driven that stretch of road hundreds of times in all conditions. Why would he lose control on this occasion? The most plausible theory seemed to be that Steve had swerved to avoid another vehicle coming downhill around one of the blind curves. But there was no hard evidence, and no motorist had stepped forward to admit involvement.

Nonetheless, that theory drew even more attention to my unwitting role in the catastrophe. Again, a few seconds give or take at any moment would have spared him—if Steve hadn't stopped to talk in front of Kenny's house; if I had gone home from the party with Kenny and spared Pre his errand. These questions burned in my brain, too, inducing a case of survivor's guilt even heavier than the one I felt in relation to my siblings and Dr. Sam. But at the same time, also similar to my experience with my father's abuse, I realized that guilt was useless and ultimately self-indulgent.

During my boyhood beatings, as Dr. Sam snorted and heaved and Felix the Cat winked obscenely at me from my father's tattoo, I realized that I was innocent—the darkness had nothing to do with me. And so it was now. I stood at the heart of the tragedy—I served as the unwitting catalyst setting the whole terrible chain of events in motion—but there was nothing I could have done to change what happened.

My job now was to let go of the what-ifs. I stayed in Eugene for about a week after the accident. Along with Kenny Moore and Bill Bowerman, I eulogized Pre at the memorial service held at Hayward Field, and then drove down to the funeral and interment in Coos Bay. Having spent so much time around him recently, I had a good idea of Pre's goals and thinking, what he had hoped for himself and for the sport in general.

His death opened a void—how could we start to fill it, how would he want us to respond? One thing was certain. I recalled all those interval sessions where we had pushed each other to the edge, all those races where we had rooted as hard for our friends as we had for ourselves. If Pre were alive, he would have told me to just get over my guilt and deal with my emotions by running harder.

Soon after the tragedy, people started comparing Steve Prefontaine's life and death to that of James Dean's. I agreed that the athlete and the actor projected the same fire and intensity and charisma, but there was one difference. James Dean came out of a Hollywood world of fabricated myth and professionally crafted legend. Steve Prefontaine didn't have an inauthentic bone in his body. Every time out, he put everything he had on the line.

+ + +

Although the season opened in tragedy and Pre's shocking death continued to reverberate around Eugene, the summer of 1975 brought high tides and green grass to the nascent American distance-running movement. In Falmouth, Massachusetts, on Cape Cod, a gregarious barkeep and runner named Tommy Leonard had watched my gold medal marathon run in Munich and got inspired to hold a road race between two of his favorite taverns. Tommy had connections to the Greater Boston Track Club coached by Bill Squires—Tommy was connected to *everybody*—and that August the cream of the Boston running community, along with 100 or so citizen-runners, showed up at the beach for the inaugural Falmouth Road Race. Tommy invited me to run and afforded me a raucous welcome. I had a blast at Falmouth and ran well, edging a talented local guy who had won the Boston Marathon the previous April and whom everybody was starting to mention as my challenger and rival: Bill Rodgers.

A few weeks after Falmouth, Bill and I engaged at an even more intense battle at a race called the Virginia 10-Miler. Bill had a knack for hanging around through all of my surges; every time I thought I had put him away, he kept coming back on my shoulder. Finally, with about a mile to go, we looked at one another and decided to call off the battle and go for a tie; during that era, when you weren't competing for prize money, races sometimes ended in a tie. We crossed the line with our hands joined. By AAU rules, however, only one person could be called the winner. Somehow they decided on Bill. I didn't mind, as long as our times both went down as the same. So the summer of 1975 began my long association with Bill Rodgers.

Bill thrived on racing the way I thrived on training. But his fierceness and focus matched mine, showing that there are different routes up the marathon mountain. In terms of skill and talent, Bill and I were equals. In a race, he had this amazing bulldog ability to hang on, hang on, and eventually wear you down. He would never let that invisible thread stretch beyond 10 meters, and his surges were long and sustained, differing from the quick explosive way in which I would separate from the pack. Bill would hurt you slowly. He was relentless. From the start, Bill Rodgers and I respected one another, but we did not bond in the way I had bonded with my earlier competitors—Kenny and Jack and Pre. Bill and I never trained together, we never socialized, but we were always aware of each other.

Meanwhile, in terms of shoe sponsorship, I decided to make a change from Asics and Adidas and go with Nike, an Oregon-based company born in Eugene—the Nike that Steve Prefontaine had believed in to the extent that he embodied its spirit. The Nike of Bill Bowerman and Phil Knight (in the early days Bowerman preceded Knight when you thought about the company); of Jeff Johnson, Geoff Hollister, and Rob Strasser, the lawyer—the men who had been at the party in Eugene on the night that Pre delivered me to Kenny Moore's house and then drove on to his death. Nike had conceived an advertising campaign around Pre. He was their first sponsored athlete, their first charismatic, hip, passionate, fierce surrogate and symbol.

As long as Pre was alive, there was room for only one Nike-sponsored runner. Steve used to pitch me on becoming a Nike guy, and I was interested. If the shoes were good enough for Pre, they would be okay with me, and I liked the whole Eugene vibe—Hayward and Bowerman and the fans clapping rhythmically as you ran past the home grandstand—and I liked Hollister and Johnson. I was tempted but since it was Pre's turf, I demurred. But now that he was gone and now that Phil Knight himself wanted to explore the possibility of signing me to an endorsement deal as Nike's featured runner at the Montreal Games, I was ready to listen.

The Nike execs invited me to a meeting. I sat in a room with Johnson, Hollister, and Strasser and the chairman, Phil Knight. Hollister and Strasser did most of the talking—they were positive, persuasive, and big, knowledgeable fans of my work. Geoff promised me a terrific pair of racing flats with a swoosh, which he would design personally, for me to wear during the Olympic Marathon. Phil Knight sat to the side, watching, listening, and not saying much. Strasser offered a good deal with favorable terms. I said sure, we shook hands, and there were smiles all around.

The Nike 5 were a group I admired. Bill Bowerman, their mentor, was an honorable man and the best running-shoe designer on the planet. I knew that Bowerman made Kenny Moore's shoes,

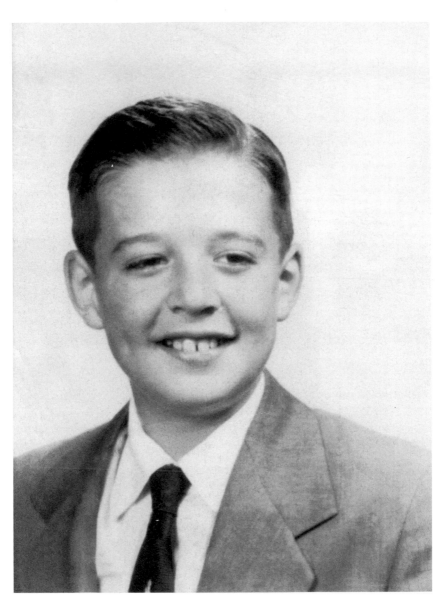

1957 class picture (*courtesy of Frank Shorter*)

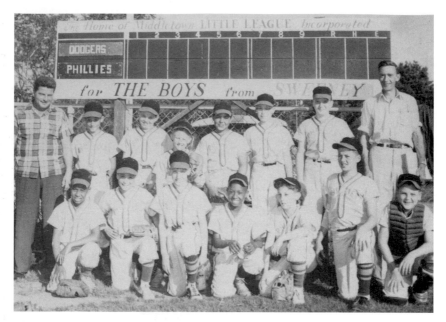

1958 Middletown Little League Phillies team photo. I am in the first row, second from the right. I played 1st base and batted cleanup. I had yet to discover running. (*courtesy of Frank Shorter*)

1959 Cathedral Choir School of St. John the Divine (now named The Cathedral School) school picture, grades 4 to 8. I am standing in the third row, third from the right. We had choir rehearsal twice a day and sang in the cathedral four or five times per week. (*courtesy of Frank Shorter*)

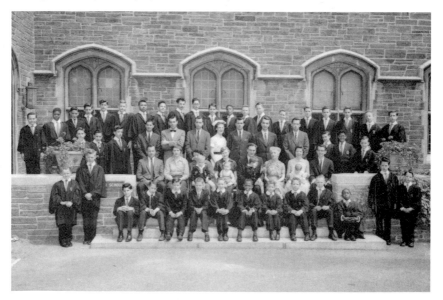

1959 Shorter/Chappell family in the backyard at 46 Highland Avenue, Middletown, New York. First row in the grass, left to right: siblings Chris, Amie, Nanette, Mary, Susan, Sam, and Frank (kneeling). Second row seated, left to right: maternal uncle John Chappell with his son, Steve, my maternal grandmother, Ida Chappell Thorpe, and her sister Dot Merrill. Standing: my mother, Katherine, holding sister, Barbara. (*courtesy of Frank Shorter*)

Photo from 1960 taken by my sister Susan. I liked to find quiet places around the house where I could read undisturbed and just think. (*courtesy of Frank Shorter*)

1963 Mount Hermon School cross-country team; we were the New England Prep School League Cross Country Champions. I'm at the far right, and Coach Warren Hall is at center. This was my first running team. (*courtesy of Frank Shorter*)

1964 Mount Hermon School home cross-country course with teammate and roommate Eugene Harris. That fall I set a course record in every race I ran and won the New England Prep School League Championships. (*courtesy of Frank Shorter*)

1965 Mount Hermon
School yearbook
photo. (*courtesy of
Frank Shorter*)

1965 Mount Hermon School
graduation picture, on
campus with my paternal
grandmother, Ethel Shorter,
and my brother Chris. The
yellow ribbon signifies
graduating cum laude, that is,
with honors. Next academic
and athletic stop: Yale.
(*courtesy of Frank Shorter*)

1965 senior year varsity cross-country captain photo for the Yale yearbook. I finished 19th in the NCAA Cross-Country Championship race that year and was named an All-American for the first time. (*courtesy Yale University Sports Information Department*)

1970 National Cross-Country
Championships in Chicago.
This was the first of four
consecutive wins for me in this
event. The Florida Track Club
won the team championship.
(*courtesy of Donald Sparks*)

Jack Bacheler, my mentor, finished
second in the same race behind me,
the student. We trained together
through the 1972 Olympic
Marathon, where Jack finished 9th.
(*courtesy of Donald Sparks*)

September 10, 1972. Munich Olympics Marathon victory ceremony during the playing of the the US national anthem. From left to right: Karel Lismont of Belgium (silver medal, 2:14:31), Frank Shorter of the United States (gold medal, 2:12:19.8), and Mamo Wolde of Ethiopia (bronze medal, 2:15:08). I felt proud to be an American athlete representing our ever-improving running community, proving that we could be competitive on the world scene. (*courtesy UPI*)

Walking off the infield after receiving the gold medal and saluting American fans who were cheering for me. I did not know whether to wave or clench my fist, so I did something in-between. (*courtesy AP Images*)

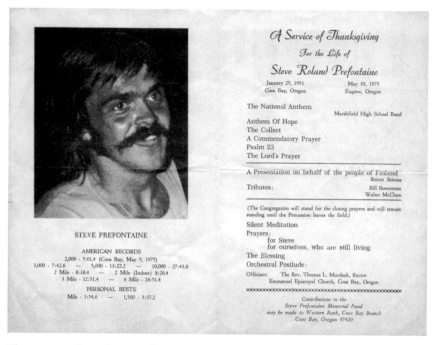

The program from Steve Prefontaine's (Pre's) memorial service in Coos Bay, Oregon, days after his death on May 25, 1975. His hometown was grieving. (*courtesy of Frank Shorter*)

The entire state of Oregon was in mourning, but Pre's impact on the sport he loved was destined to grow. (*courtesy of Frank Shorter*)

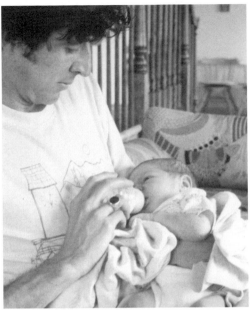

Feeding my first son, Alex, at home in Boulder, Colorado, 1979. The paradigm of my life was shifting over from primarily running to family and business. (*courtesy of Frank Shorter*)

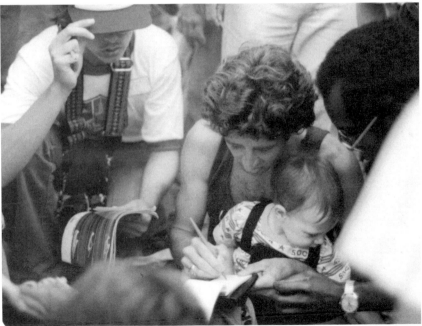

Signing autographs after the 1980 Olympic Marathon Trials while holding Alex. I knew as we sat there that it had been my final attempt to run a major marathon as hard and as fast as I could. My mind and body had told me that at about mile 15 of the 26.2 mile race. My intuition was confirmed by my 24th-place finish. (*courtesy of Frank Shorter*)

To Frank
with best wishes, Bill Clinton

1995 White House Oval Office photo with President Bill Clinton after he had run with me and Bill Rodgers. We would both now like to run as fast as we ran the 5K that day. (*courtesy of Frank Shorter*)

Deutsches Krebsforschungszentrum
Forschungsschwerpunkt 1 *Krebsentstehung und Differenzierung*
German Cancer Research Center
Research Program 1 *Cell Differentiation and Carcinogenesis*

Frank Shorter
3800 Pleasant Ridge Road
Boulder, Colo 80302

001 303 449 2284

Abteilung für Zellbiologie 0110
Division for Cell Biology 0110

Prof. Dr. Werner W. Franke

Im Neuenheimer Feld 280
D-69120 Heidelberg,FRG
Fax no.: ++49 (6221) 42-3404
Telephone Secretary: ++49 (6221) 42-3400
Telephone Direct: ++49 (6221) 42-3212

Heidelberg, January 16, 1999

Dear Mr. Shorter,

in answer to your fax inquiry of January 5 /15 I am herewith sending you the relevant pages from the protocols of the governmental commission evaluating and guiding the GDR Doping since 1974 (attached). Please note that this is from top-secret material and that the pages I am sending are officially authorized by the Federal office responsible for the treatment of secret governmental files of the former GDR: This is indicated by the Federal stamp (rectangle with "BStU" and number). Page 105, which mentions the name of Waldemar Cierpinski - code number 62 - is listed in an appendix to a top-secret note from Feb. 4, 1976 (starting on p. 99). This indicates that several middle and long distance runners already in the 70s were part of the doping program of the GDR and that Cierpinski was already on androgenic steroids in 1976.

Yours sincerely

Dr. Werner W. Franke

Some evidence relating to the long-suspected East German State–sponsored doping system for all athletes competing abroad from the early 1970s until the Berlin wall was torn down in 1989. On my own initiative I had requested a meeting with Dr. Werner Franke when I read he would be in Colorado Springs at the Olympic Training Center in January 1998. At that meeting he assured me he had some documents to send me. He was true to his word. I leave it to the reader to evaluate. (*courtesy of Frank Shorter*)

THE WHITE HOUSE

WASHINGTON

February 22, 1999

Mr. Frank Shorter
3800 Pleasant Ridge Road
Boulder, Colorado 80301

Dear Frank:

    Thank you so much for your kind letter.
I'm delighted that you are already working with
General McCaffrey. I know he and his staff will
benefit from your experience and wise counsel.

    You and Paddy have my best wishes.

Sincerely,

Bill Clinton

President Bill Clinton's reply to my letter dated several days prior in which I had thanked him for supporting one of his Cabinet members, General Barry McCaffrey, in the General's efforts at the ONDCP (Office of National Drug Control Policy) to bring about the creation of USADA (the United States Anti-Doping Agency). In my opinion, the White House's support of this major change in policy with regard to the international use of performance-enhancing drugs is the only reason anything could have happened. (*courtesy of Frank Shorter*)

Sports world

Shorter, Rodgers to enter new Hall

Former U.S. Olympians **Frank Shorter** and **Bill Rodgers** are among the first five inductees into the National Distance Running Hall of Fame in Utica.

Also to be inducted into the Hall on July 11 are **Ted Corbitt, Joan Benoit Samuelson** and **Katharine Switzer**.

Shorter, a native of Middletown, N.Y., was a five-time U.S. champion in the 10,000 meters, Olympic gold-medal winner in 1972 and silver medalist in 1976. He is a regular participant in the Orange Classic 10k in Middletown.

Rodgers is a four-time winner of the Boston and New York marathons and was a member of the 1976 U.S. Olympic team.

Corbitt set U.S. records for the 25-, 40-, and 50-mile marathons and was a member of the 1952 U.S. Olympic team. Benoit Samuelson won the first Olympic women's marathon in 1984.

Switzer was the first woman to officially run the Boston Marathon and won the 1974 New York Marathon.

The Hall of Fame is being created with the cooperation of Hamilton College. Voting was done by race directors, Hall of Fame officials and Road Runners Club of America members.

All but one of the inductees mentioned in this 1998 newspaper story are household names to runners who participated in the first wave of the running boom in the 1970s. Ted Corbitt, who labored in obscurity in the 1950s, deserves equal recognition as a pioneer of the sport. (*courtesy of Frank Shorter*)

The Shorter Track

Given in Honor of

Frank C. Shorter, Class of 1969

Olympic Gold and Silver Marathon Medalist

by

His Friend, Donald M. Roberts, Class of 1957

February 12, 2005

The pencil note reads "Frank, let me know your thoughts of this as a suggestion for a dedication plaque—Don." This totally unexpected gesture of appreciation and recognition from my friend Don Roberts still leaves me speechless. In 2004 he donated a much-needed indoor track to our alma mater with the stipulation that it be named after me. I continue to feel humbled and honored that someone would want to express his generosity through me. (*courtesy of Frank Shorter*) and those of many other University of Oregon runners. The relationship between Bowerman and Phil Knight was especially close. So when Geoff Hollister lined me up with the group, I had no reservations on any level. Bill Bowerman's spirit and expertise permeated the entire operation. Indeed, Bill had taught Geoff his shoe-making craft. That was the only personal meeting I ever had with Phil Knight. I had seen Phil at Pre's funeral service in Coos Bay but I hadn't spoken with him. In all, I had great optimism about the Nike deal.

16

The Shadow

Virtually all the distance runners on the Olympic-level circuit strongly suspected that Lasse Viren, the 1972 gold medalist in the 5000 and 10,000, was blood doping, but there was no way to prove it. There was no test for blood doping, a technique by which you drew plasma from your own body, stuck it in a refrigerator, and then returned to training. A few weeks or months later, at the opportune moment before competition, you injected the stored plasma back into your veins, which gave a huge kick to your oxygen-carrying capacity. The technique was morally and ethically wrong. Blood-doping was no different than taking an anabolic steroid, the drug of choice in the Eastern Bloc, but because you weren't injecting a synthetic drug or other foreign substance, there was no way at the time to detect it. Since officials couldn't punish behavior they couldn't prove, blood-doping wasn't even banned by the IOC. That wouldn't happen until 1984.

Why did we think Viren was blood doping? Because his performances were so uneven. Before he broke out with his double gold-medal performance at the Munich Games, he had been an average college runner at Brigham Young University, and few in the running community had heard of him—he barely raised a blip on the international radar. That was okay, as far as it went; Viren clearly possessed first-rate talent, and he'd apparently timed his emergence on the world stage perfectly. Immediately after the Games, however, Viren disappeared again. He had logged nothing but mediocre performances for more than two years, which did not conform to the logic and rhythm of the sport; if you lit up the distance-running sky in 1972, you weren't going to disappear from the radar screen in 1973. Viren blamed his eclipse on injuries and illness, but those excuses rang false, especially when he magically healed as the '76 Olympics in Montreal approached.

Beyond that admittedly circumstantial evidence, there was an instinctive suspicion—an intuitive conviction—on the circuit when it came to doping. We could sense when another runner was juicing. You could see it in the jump of his stride, the fresh smile after a draining workout that would have left an honest athlete pale and trembling. You could see it in the unvarying pace as they ran beside you. They gave no sign of tiring, even as miles accumulated. When the pace intensified at the end of a race, they still didn't grow weary.

We sensed that Viren was cheating. We knew he was connected to the European apparatus of blood-doping that had originated in Finland in 1970, when doctors transformed a mediocre steeplechaser who suffered from anemia into a world-class athlete. But at the same time, Viren was living a double life of public probity and private falsehood. Viren had become a global star, a master of the sport that, more than others, was based on self-discipline and self-mastery and appeared to embody Olympian ideals of honesty and fair play. In the unthreatening Scandinavian manner, Viren even looked innocent. He was long-haired and delicate-featured, unassuming and humble. I liked the guy; when Pre and I had barnstormed around Finland the summer before, we had even crashed for a night at his place and run with him in the forest the next morning. There was no point questioning Viren's honesty, just as there was no point in questioning the honesty of our own shot-putters and hammer throwers, those 300-pound pop-muscled sumos who openly talked about anabolic dosing and who carried needles and vials in their equipment bags.

But in the eyes of many athletes, Viren and other suspected blood-dopers were cheating morally.

Juicing was nothing new in track and field, and you couldn't pretend that it was a purely foreign evil, a manifestation of cold war power politics, a totalitarian poison. In 1974, at the national track and field championships in Bakersfield, Pre and I were jogging back to the hotel with Leonard Hilton, who had just won the mile. Leonard was a country boy from Texas, who would go on to make the 1976 Olympic team at 5,000 meters. Pre and I congratulated Leonard on his victory. He responded with a big grin.

"I couldn't have done it without those darn 'roids!" he said.

Pre and I just looked at each other and shrugged. We knew that doping was out there, but it didn't concern us. We didn't need or want the stuff. We were too wrapped up in our own system, which was clearly working.

Leonard Hilton may have needed his anabolics, and Lasse Viren may have relied on vials of plasma chilling at the back of his refrigerator in Finland, but why would I need jet juice? Even if I hadn't been winning races, doping would have taken the fun out of the sport, the bone-deep gratification of knowing how much pain and effort went into throwing down a 4:30 surge at the 10-mile post of a marathon or a 56-second 400 at the close of a 10,000.

+ + +

Louise and I were happy to be living in Boulder. She was working full-time as a librarian at an elementary school in the nearby town of Louisville. I ran long with Joe French and Bob Stone, partners in the law firm where I worked part-time.

Boulder had evolved into a featured stop on the aquarian highway. The nation's first downtown pedestrian mall was taking shape on Pearl Street, and I was accepted as a citizen who had won an Olympic Gold Medal and who had chosen to live there. Boulder is a city in which no one subculture dominates and whose inhabitants appreciate high achieving goal-setters whether they are working in academics, industry, or sports and who give them the space to do it. For Louise and me, it was all blue mornings, golden afternoons, starlit nights, and the moon lifting clear over the front range of the Rockies.

During that span I limited myself to one marathon a year—Fukuoka, whose date best fit my schedule and which continued to draw a higher-quality international field than races such as the Boston Marathon. Also, adding another marathon campaign to my carefully crafted training schedule would have disrupted my routine. In that same vein, even when training for a marathon, I never went past 20 miles on my long run. If you went past 20, you reaped diminishing returns. If you ran more than 20 on Sunday, you went into tear-down mode and wouldn't be able to log your hard-speed workout until Wednesday at the earliest. And then you wouldn't be fresh, and those hard 400s and 800s and 1200s were really the key; the pain you felt during interval workouts allowed you to embrace the same pain during a marathon. Moreover, you indexed your pace on your easy recovery miles to the pace you ran the intervals on your hard days.

Except when I was running interval repeats on the track, I always worked by perceived effort rather than the stopwatch. I strove for consistency. I intentionally trained so that if I wanted to, I could try for a PR at distances ranging from the mile to the marathon at any time of year. But at the same time there were subtle shadings to each day's work, variations depending on weather and terrain and training partners. Running was a constantly absorbing challenge, and it was all great fun.

My life was coming together, and in the clarifying light of those days, I never gave a thought to the shadow of my father. I had not seen him since that awkward reunion at the Olympic celebration in Middletown in 1972, and he was no longer afflicting my sisters, brothers, or mother. Dr. Sam's persecution of Michael, my little brother with Down syndrome, was too much for even Katherine to endure. In 1975, my mother divorced my father, and he returned to Middletown, where he was revered and where he had secretly committed his most grievous crimes.

+ + +

After four straight years of winning the race, I did not run the Fukuoka Marathon in December 1975. I was in my physical prime, and I had my system down to the model of consistency that had always been my goal. I had now been competing on a world-class level for five years. I felt like I understood the marathon and had developed a system of training that was uniquely mine. There was still a world left to learn, but how much longer could I sustain this energy, this mental, physical, and psychological commitment, the endless skein of 20-mile training days and withering twice-a-week intervals? More specifically, how long until I finally suffered the defining injury that was every elite distance runner's lot?

In 1973 I had developed a stress fracture in my left foot, but it quickly healed. I had had no significant physical issues since then, but how long would my luck hold? Studying the history of the sport, I determined that five to seven years—two Olympiads— were the longest that a distance runner could reasonably expect to compete at a world-class level. My window was still open, but soon, inevitably, it would start to close. I wanted to find out if I could run even better on my second time around at the Olympics. In August 1975 I had logged my PR for the 10,000. I sensed that I should prepare for only two more marathons, the Olympic trials and the Olympic race. I had nothing more to prove—not much more to learn—by running in Fukuoka again. I stayed in Boulder all through December and January, hitting out a 10-week block of uninterrupted training.

On February 19, 1976, I ran a 6 × 800 interval session at the fieldhouse on the Colorado campus, at the time, still the only indoor track in the United States lying above 5,000 feet elevation (another reason to love Boulder, along with its 300 sunny days a year). Unlike many distance runners, I always liked training and racing indoors. The indoor venue concentrated the energy and intensity; at times it seemed as if a big invisible hand were pulling me around the track. I began that workout feeling as light as an aspen leaf shimmering in the Rocky Mountain breeze.

I was one of the favorites to win a second consecutive Olympic Marathon. The world was changing—the 1960s-spawned counter-culture was fading, although many of its precepts—from passing fashions like long hair to fundamental achievements such as female empowerment—had gone mainstream. Distance running had been folded into that mix: a new way of moving and knowing. The boom was building, and due to my win at Munich, the media labeled me as its father. I didn't care about any of that. I just stuck to my training. I kept trying to get it right.

I began to feel that dull ache—more pressure than pain. But that sort of discomfort was my companion, my true training partner. I jogged my 60 seconds of rest and flowed into the third rep—four hard laps around the 200-meter track. I had hit out two laps and was sailing into the third when I felt something pop in my left ankle.

I knew right away it was major—I felt a snap, a shout of pain—but it quickly faded, and I kept on running. Unfortunately, a serious athlete's first response to injury is almost always denial. Despite the intensity and duration of my training, I had never suffered a major injury, and I didn't know how to deal with it. So I just kept running. I didn't have time to be injured. I just backed off for an instant and then adjusted my form to take the pressure off the foot. The Olympic Marathon Trials were scheduled for May in Eugene. I ran a few decent track races before them. My training seemed to be going well, but in April a cyst or lump formed at the spot of my injury. The doc would drain it, and I went back to training, but the cyst would form again, and the cycle would repeat.

I was dinged. As the Hawaiians say, this was my Big Kahuna. Every runner gets it sooner or later. What matters is how you deal with it. You can adjust, but your biomechanics get permanently affected. The arc goes downhill after that. Specifically, my injury was to the navicular bone of my left ankle. It started as a stress fracture, but the big problem, the main problem, was the subdural cyst that developed as the fracture healed. The lump formed on my ankle. The cyst bothered me more than the stress fracture itself.

But the injury didn't seem to affect speed training. I didn't let it alter my routine. I could not take the 6 weeks off from running that is the minimum requirement for healing this sort of injury. There were only 10 crucial weeks until the trials, so I kept hitting it. I didn't think about the injury, and I felt as if I was in good shape—great shape. But I wouldn't know for sure until I submitted to the stress of the marathon.

In May I traveled to Eugene for the Olympic Marathon Trials. For the first time, the marathon comprised a separate event, preceding the rest of the track-and-field trials by several weeks in order to give the three marathon qualifiers more time to recover and prepare for the Games. It was my first time in town since Pre's death a year earlier, and his absence was almost palpable. Now my main man and rival, the other contender on the scene, was Bill Rodgers. By now Bill was running really well, and he and I were the clear favorites. I had beaten him at a 10-K road race in Ohio earlier that month, but that didn't prove anything; more so than I, Bill specialized in the marathon and saved his best for the distance. In April he had won the first of his five Boston Marathon titles and was already known as Boston Billy. Indeed, Bill was developing a fan following similar to that of Pre's (I lacked those guys' common touch; I might have been "the father of the boom," but I'd never attracted such a following).

At the trials race, Bill and I broke away from the pack early. We ran together, sharing the lead, much in the way that Kenny and I had shared the lead in this race four years earlier. We knew we had our spots on the team locked up, so there was no point trying to race each other. We hit the halfway point at 1:04:50, and we both realized how far ahead we were. We slowed down and covered the second half in 1:07. We decided that we were going to do the same thing as at that Virginia 10 Miler and finish in a tie.

A half-mile out from the finish line, however, Bill slowed down and started to limp with a hamstring injury. I slowed down with him, but he told me he was okay and could make it to the finish. He waved and told me to go on ahead. I did so but didn't push it too hard because I didn't want to show him up. I won the race in 2:11:51, Bill finished second in 2:11:59, and Don Kardong, a Stanford graduate who would later found the Lilac Bloomsday Run in his native Spokane, Washington, claimed the third Olympic spot. My ankle held up. All through the race I never thought about my injury.

The track and field trials followed in June, again at Hayward Field. Pre's absence, especially in the field for the 5000, produced an ache sharper than the pain from the cyst in my damaged ankle. Pilgrims were already starting to leave flowers, old running shoes, and full beer cans up at the rock where Pre had fatally crashed his sports car just over a year earlier. I kept away from the makeshift shrine and declined most media interviews, conserving my energy for the 10,000 meters.

At the start of my international career, back at the Pan American Games in '71, the 10 had been my focus and the marathon my backup. Now my identity was fused to the marathon, and the 10 was strictly prelude. Still, I won the final in a fast 27:55.45, beating the talented Craig Virgin, a runner from Indiana who would later set the American record in the distance and win the world cross-country title.

If my ankle was suspect, given the likely presence of blood doping so were the prospects of a level playing field for the 10,000 meters. I also had a gut feeling that I was subtly losing my fitness. Instead of again doubling in the 10 and marathon, I decided to focus solely on defending my Olympic title in the marathon. All I could do was copy the approach I'd taken with the Black September killers in Munich. I would run my marathon and not give the shadow a thought.

17

Mystery Man

I spent the entire summer of 1976 in Boulder. It was the summer of the American bicentennial, the summer when Jimmy Carter was running for president against Gerald Ford, who had succeeded the disgraced Richard Nixon. The order was rapidly fading, as Bob Dylan had sung in the 1960s, but except for shaving off my mustache, I followed the same routine as in my buildup to the '72 Games. Due to my injury, I wasn't able to train quite as hard; I realized I needed to dole out my energy and time carefully. My tactics would be the same as in Munich: Go out with the lead pack, throw a midrace surge, and hold on. No secrets or surprises this time. The other runners would know what was coming, but it shouldn't make a difference. If another challenger were out there in the international marathon scene, he would have shown himself by now. I truly felt that Bill Rodgers was my main competition, but due to his hamstring injury, he wouldn't be on top of his game in Montreal. Once again, I felt I was capable of finishing in the top three. I was confident that I'd be ready to do my best when it mattered most.

The Games began in late July. A week or so before the opening ceremony, Louise and I drove to the Olympic team assembly area in Plattsburgh, New York. We visited relatives on my mother's side of the family in Canton, New York, and then drove north across the border. The nation of Canada and the province of Quebec had invested heavily in hosting the Olympics, building a new stadium, hoping to show its best to the world in the way Munich had tried to show its best at those ill-fated 1972 Games. But times had changed, and the world was a colder place. The modern Olympic movement had lost its last vestiges of innocence after the Munich Massacre.

We have never quite recovered from Munich, and we'll never likely regain the energy and idealism that, despite lapses and excesses, defined the Olympic movement from 1896 until the moment the Black September killers climbed over the fence in the Olympic Village. Not all of the changes were negative—it didn't hurt that a strain of professionalism now ran through the Games and that athletes from the West could now train with a modicum of security and comfort, leveling the playing field somewhat with the state-supported Eastern Bloc performers. But in general there was a new air of cynicism and exploitation; athletes were no longer free agents. We felt like pawns being moved around by the masters of war, or, to mix metaphors, like ships being blown across uncharted waters by the winds of cold war geopolitics.

From the perspective of an American distance runner, the Montreal Games presented an especially mixed bag. Due to the geopolitics, the East African runners would be absent; their nations were boycotting the Games to protest the apartheid regime of South Africa and the general phenomenon of colonialism that had blighted the developing world. On the other hand, the Soviet and Eastern Bloc athletes would be out in force, minions of the anabolic-fueled propaganda machine and the medal-count arms race. The Western European and antipodal runners were always strong. America in general was suffering the effect of the post-Vietnam, post-'60s malaise and hangover. We had lost a measure of confidence in ourselves, grown ambivalent about our power, and our Olympic team reflected this slide. Our traditionally dominant track-and-field team had only three clear gold medal favorites: Edwin Moses, a 400-meter hurdler; the decathlete Bruce Jenner; and myself.

And now, of course, I could no longer slip in and out of the athlete's village, anonymously riding the metro. I was the defending Olympic Marathon champion. My photo had appeared on national magazine covers, and in 1972 I had won the prestigious Sullivan Award, which goes to the year's outstanding American amateur athlete. My previously arcane discipline, the marathon, had sprouted into a trend, a movement, a sport, and a pastime, and I had emerged as one of the movement's role models. Across the nation, thousands of ordinary citizens now trained virtually as hard as I did. Both from a spectator and participant perspective, the marathon was no longer a virgin, unexplored continent. Similar to the Munich Marathon, where I ran with a figurative bull's-eye on my back, I now ran as a target that the public and my competitors could key on.

I preferred anonymity and found it at an inn rented by Nike just outside Montreal. Geoff Hollister hosted Louise and me. I also had a room at the Olympic athletes' village, which turned out to be fortunate. Louise stayed mostly at the inn, while I spent most nights at my room in the village. But I would visit her frequently, training on the roads near the inn. Still, the attention wasn't altogether a bad thing. I could deploy it as a psychological advantage. I knew my opponents were watching me, just as those Eastern Bloc runners had been watching back in Fukuoka in 1971, when I stepped off the bus during the course tour and ran those hard kilometers back to the hotel. Now, in Montreal, I did not use public transportation, but Louise drove me out to Mount Royal, a tall hill jutting out at mile 11 of the course (technically you weren't supposed to have steep inclines on an Olympic marathon course; we suspected that organizers had inserted the hill because Jerome Drayton, the Canadian hope for a medal in the event, was strong on the hills). I ran my 5-K time trial over the mountain, hitting my splits, in dress rehearsal for the surge I'd deliver during the actual race. I didn't care if my competitors knew what was coming. If they could respond to it, more power to them. Meanwhile, my time trial at Mount Royal gave them something to think about.

Due to my standing in the sport and the fact that I'd decided not to run the event, ABC invited me to provide commentary for its coverage of the 10,000 meters. Viren won as expected; again, the graceful, lithe, long-haired Finn flashed across the line, looking more like a rocker than a jock, prevailing in a contemplative individual sport in which you competed more against yourself than other runners or the clock. I wasn't about to say anything about the shadow hanging over Viren or disabuse fans in their hope that an alternative sort of sports hero had emerged. Indeed, I had also been placed in this alternative camp—even though my greatest pleasure was cleaning the clock of Harvard rivals in the smelly dark IC4A field houses of the cold Northeast.

During a commercial break I turned to Erich Segal, my old Yale prof, who had returned to the broadcast booth after his uproarious stint at the Munich Games. That pale guy running in the pack, holding a strong pace, could be a good marathoner, I said. We looked him up in the program. His name was Carlos Lopes, and he ran for Portugal.

+ + +

August 9, 1976. The morning of my second Olympic Marathon. Four years earlier, on September 10, 1972, despite the cataclysm of the Munich Massacre and the fact that I was a virtual unknown sleeping on the concrete floor of a dorm-room balcony, I had woken up knowing I was in rhythm, that I was getting something right. Today, in Montreal, I tried to tell myself the same thing. I tried to take confidence in my additional four years of purposeful, thoughtful training, in my string of marathon and track victories around the globe, in my worldwide number-one ranking in the marathon, and my successful time trial over Mount Royal just a few days earlier, but I knew that something was off. I wasn't quite in sync. I sensed that even though I'd prepared to my utmost, I had fallen a centimeter out of step with the marathon gods, the forces beyond my control. But that's why you run your hardest workouts on the day they are scheduled, even if you're feeling terrible. Dealing with feeling less than my best on race day was also something I'd practiced.

I followed my ritual and routine: the prerace meal of toast, fruit, and coffee; the calm trip over to the Olympic Stadium. Such was my focus that I didn't even notice the gray skies and the humid drape of August eastern rain showers. I went into the holding area with Rodgers, Kardong, and the other runners, sensing them giving me appraising glances. I arranged the items in my gear bag, preparing to go out to the fenced-off area where we could complete our final warm-up.

Everything was in order, but for some reason I decided to break with my usual practice and put on my racing flats before heading out to the track; in my previous marathons, I would wait until moments before the starting gun to lace up my racing shoes. It wasn't a conscious decision to change my routine, and for a moment I considered changing back to my trainers. But that seemed overly fussy; I wasn't superstitiously committed to an exact sequence of preparation. I depended on routine, but I wasn't weird about it. That seemingly inconsequential break in my ritual, however, turned out to be crucial.

To review my arrangement with Nike: I was the second high-profile competitive runner to wear the company's shoes. The first was Steve Prefontaine, who inspired Phil Knight (who had also run for Bill Bowerman at the University of Oregon) to grow Nike, originally known as Blue Ribbon Sports, from a small-time niche enterprise selling knock-off Japanese shoes at high school track meets into a legitimate business with an exotic, resonant brand name.

My deal with Nike was a straightforward proposition, and in those strict amateur days, there was no money involved—at least not for the athlete. The company execs wanted me to wear a pair of Nike racing flats during my Olympic Marathon. The Nike swoosh was in its infancy, and my displaying it to a global TV audience would help raise brand awareness. Of course, the shoe was the one indispensable piece of equipment that any runner employed. At the Munich Games, my racing flats had been custom-made by the top designer from Adidas, the German shoe company that then dominated the athletic-shoe market. Those shoes had fit so perfectly, I wasn't even aware of them as I made my surge at the Nymphenburg Castle and glided through the English Garden on the way to the stadium: the highest compliment you could pay a pair of shoes.

But I had faith that Nike could make just as good a shoe, because Bill Bowerman had done so for Pre and Kenny Moore and other University of Oregon runners.

I ran in the racing flats a couple of times in the days before the race and took them to the starting line at the stadium. The shoes felt fine. Geoff Hollister had designed them himself with my input and approval. Our goal and shared focus (too narrow a focus, as it turned out) was to produce the lightest pair of racing flats in history. Geoff found an extremely light but strong mesh material that had never been used before on performance athletic shoes. I wanted the lightest possible shoes in order to gain a psychological edge and agreed to give the prototype design a try. Looking back, it seems a rather unwise decision, because only days remained before the race.

Neither Geoff nor I thought the material would perform differently when glued to the sole of the shoe. For some reason, however, the same glue that bonded so reliably in all makes and models of training and racing shoes failed in these superlight, custom-made flats.

Although I had no reason to doubt the shoes, I had practiced the due diligence of an Olympic runner. Just in case there was an unforeseen problem with the Nike prototypes, I had arranged for a backup pair of racing flats to be shipped from Boulder to Montreal (those shoes were manufactured by another company; I have very narrow feet and Nike's production-line racing flats were too wide for me to race properly). However, I left the backup pair in my room in the athletes' village because the prototype shoes so skillfully designed by Geoff had worked fine during several training runs I'd logged over the previous few days. Indeed, since Phil Knight and I had shaken hands on our deal earlier that year, I had worn nothing but Nike shoes.

Just before the start of the marathon, in the warm-up area outside the stadium, I jogged back and forth in my racing flats. The shoes felt different; they felt strangely loose. I retied and tightened the laces but they still felt loose. I looked down and saw that the sole of the right shoe had separated from the upper and my bare sole was open to the air. For some unknown reason the glue had failed to hold; the shoe had fallen apart.

Instead of feeling panic, I immediately thought of what my options might be. Was there time to rush back to my room at the athletes' village and return with my backup racing flats? That didn't seem possible—there was now less than half an hour until the starting gun.

You know that nightmare in which you're trying to get someplace crucially important but you lack the crucially important element—a pair of pants, a set of keys—necessary to complete the mission? Well, in the moments before the 1976 Olympic Marathon, I was living out this nightmare. But I couldn't wake up and have it go away.

It was a crisis, and yet I felt strangely calm. I didn't know how it would happen, but I knew I was going to make it. I looked down again at the ripped and flapping shoe, then looked up to see a man—or was it an angel?—standing on the other side of the chain-link fence separating the warm-up area from the stadium concourse; since Munich, Olympic security had improved significantly. I recognized him—it was Bruce McDonald, a US racewalking coach, who happened to be staying in the same suite of rooms in village as I was. Bruce would have a key to get in my room!

I rushed over to the fence and explained my predicament. Bruce, bless his heart, booked away at a dead sprint to retrieve my backup racing flats. I waited in the warm-up area. Instead of cursing my bad luck, I reverted to my default mode of dealing with stress: movement. I jogged back and forth in my training shoes. For some reason, I remained calm. I felt confident that this would work out.

Finally, after all the other runners had gone into the stadium and I was alone in the warm-up area, I was visited by a wondrous sight: Bruce skidding to a stop and chucking my back-up pair of racing flats over the chain-link fence. There were now less than 5 minutes until the starting gun. I laced up the flats, ran out onto the track and across the infield, and took my place on the starting line, as if nothing untoward had transpired.

Looking back at that moment, I might have felt that fate was messing with me—that the skein of unfavorable signs beginning with Pre's death the year before and encompassing my ankle injury and the specter of blood-doping was continuing. I might well have thought that something was amiss; that, in contrast to my experience at Munich '72, when all the breaks fell my way, I wasn't quite in rhythm.

But I didn't feel that way. I can truthfully say that I remained confident and focused on the job at hand. Just as I had learned to run fast when I was tired, I had learned to go hard on bad days, when I was feeling weary or off-kilter. Again, it was back to the fundamentals of the sport: Work through the finish. Don't change your plan due to unfavorable interior or exterior weather. And only now, as the gun cracked, as I shot to the front and claimed the inside lane to save me a few meters, as we circled the track once before exiting the arena to the streets of Montreal, did I take note of the actual weather. A steady drizzle spattered the Tartan surface of the inside lane. The roof of the gleaming new stadium, soon to be resented by the people of Quebec because its construction costs accrued a mountain of crushing public debt, sheltered the outside lanes. The crowd cheered lustily as we exited the arena. It was the final day of track-and-field competition but not the final day of the Games.

Following my custom, I ran hard through the early miles, setting an honest pace, part of a lead group of 9 or 10 athletes that quickly separated from the rest of the pack. Bill Rodgers and Don Kardong were among the leaders, and so was Lasse Viren, running his first marathon, attempting to repeat the feat of his countryman Paavo Nurmi, who at the 1948 Games won gold medals in all three endurance events, the 5, the 10, and the marathon. Viren had just won the 10 yesterday, so a win today didn't seem feasible, but the women of the East German swim team, breaking record after record in the pool, had proved that, through better chemistry, anything was possible.

The shadow was present, something was off, but as the miles accrued, I felt more and more like myself, more and more confident that my training would bear out and my battle-tested plan would again yield fruit. We clipped along at well under a 5-minute pace, passing the first 10 kilometers in under 30 minutes. That was a world record pace, but we couldn't maintain that over the second half of the course, which carried over Mount Royal, where I would launch my surge.

The other runners knew what was coming, but could they do anything about it? No other marathoner could approach my 10-K speed, except for Viren. I had a great deal of respect for Bill Rodgers. I knew back in '75 after his first New York City victory, that he was legitimate. Temperamentally, Bill and I were opposites, as he quite often seemed out of focus. And while I knew that if healthy, Bill would be vying for the gold, but he was nursing that sore hamstring, and I suspected he would eventually fade.

I had my own injury to contend with. My foot seemed to be holding up (and so were my replacement pair of racing flats), as the lead pack probed into the back nine of the course. I don't remember the rain as a factor. I looked over at Bill. He normally ran with a beautiful lilting light-footed stride, but today he wasn't flowing. I knew he was struggling. And how about Viren? The entire race he'd been shadowing me, keying off me, never stepping up and sharing the lead in the manner of Kenny Moore or Jack Bacheler or another honorable marathoner. So I started to mess with him, veering in and out at the water stops, using the other guys as a screen, hiding from Viren, whose head would snap around in alarm and confusion until he finally found me. I felt good about that.

As we approached the take-off point for my surge, that's how the dynamic of the lead pack played out. I was running my own race, but I was aware of my rivals, tracking them in the manner that a radar operator traces the presence of ships sailing in the vicinity. They weren't an immediate threat; they only posed a danger if I lost sight of them. I briefly thought of Carlos Lopes, the Portuguese runner I had noticed in the 10,000 meters. He wasn't among the lead pack. All seemed in order. At my appointed spot at the base of Mount Royal, I launched my surge.

I threw down a 4:40 mile, spurting away from Bill and the rest of the lead pack, except for one man, a pale fair-haired runner who looked a lot like Lopes, but I couldn't be sure. From the moment I first noticed him, I felt puzzled. At that point of a marathon, no one is fresh. You look for fatigue, but this runner showed no weariness. He flew up on my shoulder like the bad guy in a movie car chase. And there this fellow stayed, demonstrating continued odd behavior for an elite marathoner.

He displayed no trace of his own pacing or effort or strategy. When I accelerated, he did the same. When I slowed for a few strides, he also slowed. I tried to sandbag him, slowing the pace just a hair for about a quarter mile, conveying the impression that I was tiring, and then blasting away at a near-sprint for several hundred yards. The mystery man—by now I was sure it must be Lopes—easily covered every move. It was as if invisible bands held us together. This was the shadowing tactic that Viren had attempted earlier in the race, but this guy was pulling it off.

And then, as we came down off Mount Royal in a steady summer drizzle, this mystery man stepped to the lead, opening a 10-meter gap. I answered that move, pulling back up on his shoulder, but again he took off on me. This cycle repeated three more times as the course swerved through the campus of McGill University in central Montreal. We passed the 20-mile mark, the event's notorious "wall," where the glycogen stores tap out and most marathoners, especially inexperienced ones, start to wobble and unravel. But instead of coming apart, this guy was getting stronger.

It was just the two of us, running far out in front of the rest of the pack. This was where I expected to be at this point; I was running precisely according to my plan, but I wasn't expecting company and certainly not the company of a stranger. The elite international running community wasn't that big—you knew all the significant players, at least by reputation. But my current opponent was a complete unknown. This wasn't normal; something wasn't right. Fate appeared to be messing with me again.

We went through one more hare-and-hound cycle, and then, at mile 23, the guy just powered away from me, and there was nothing I could do about it. He quickly opened a 100-meter lead, well beyond the imaginary thread by which you can hope to keep contact. We made a left turn onto the boulevard leading to the finish just as dusk started to close. I put my head down and summoned one last spurt of energy. My kick shaved perhaps 40 meters off of his lead, enough to give me some faint hope. But then, sensing my late rally, the guy glanced back over his shoulder. For an instant our eyes met. And then—I'll never forget this—he turned around and just soared away. Pick your simile—like a booster rocket—or your metaphor: He found another gear. I realized that I was beaten. I had executed my race plan, and my tender ankle had held up. Today, apparently, a better man was winning.

My opponent crossed the finish line 38 seconds ahead of me, just as I entered the tunnel leading into the stadium. I heard the roar of the crowd at the exact same moment that, four years earlier, I had heard the crowd roar in Munich when the imposter crossed the marathon finish line. And as I entered the stadium in Montreal, I encountered a strange tumult resembling the finish-line debacle in Munich. The race was over, the mystery man had won the gold medal, but the guy was still running. It wasn't a victory lap. The guy was booking. He was slamming around the track as if he were finishing an 800-meter race rather than one spanning more than 26 miles. And he wasn't making an emotional statement in the manner of John Akii-Bua, the Ugandan athlete, who after crossing the line and winning the 400-meter hurdles at the Munich Games continued running full-tilt, clearing two more hurdles out of sheer innocent joy, seeming to personify the energy coming out of a newly sovereign African nation. No. My victorious opponent was still running like a hellhound ripped from its chain. It seemed that he had misjudged the finish and thought one more lap remained in his race.

I finished my marathon in 2:10:45, almost 2 minutes faster than my time in Munich. I laced my hands behind my head and looked up at the clock. I couldn't have run any harder. That's it, I thought. I gave it all I had. I wasn't crushed. I wasn't really disappointed; I was puzzled. Finally, a full minute later, Karel Lismont and Don Kardong came into the stadium, fighting it out for the bronze; Lismont, the Belgian, won. I approached the man who I assumed to be Carlos Lopes to congratulate him on his brilliant race. As I shook his hand and got a good look at him, I realized that he wasn't Carlos Lopes. Confused, I looked up at the scoreboard, which announced that the winner was a man named Waldemar Cierpinski, competing for East Germany.

After the race I drifted around in a mildly shocked daze. I went through the drug testing protocol and stood gamely on the silver medal podium as the stern proletarian East German national anthem played. (The medal standings indeed ended dismally for the US track-and-field team; after my unexpected defeat, Edwin Moses's win in the 400-meter hurdles and Bruce Jenner's victory in the decathlon provided the only gold medals for American athletes—a stunning comedown after decades of dominance.) I submitted to an interview with ABC, during which I voiced the usual commentary, giving Cierpinski his seeming due, telling my countrymen, hey, it happens, somebody ran faster today . . . but even as I went through these motions, I was calculating the probabilities.

Something wasn't right about this. I kept seeing all those massive-shouldered East German female swimmers who'd been racking up world-record, gold medal–winning performances more profusely than Mark Spitz had in Munich; I kept seeing Waldemar Cierpinski looking back over his shoulder at me, then taking off as if he'd been shot from a cannon. A quick check on the guy's résumé yielded suspicious info: one 2:20 marathon the year before, a few decent steeplechase races, but no evidence of the extensive apprenticeship required of an honest world-class marathoner.

But there was no solid evidence that the East German team was doing something underhanded. There was nothing I could say, nothing I could do. I left the stadium and met Louise. We broke camp in Montreal and drove in thoughtful silence to her cousin's house in Canton, New York. I remember the car—a Fiat sedan. I needed to process and reframe the Olympic Marathon; evaluate it so I could move forward. I knew what had happened. Something of high value had been stolen, not just from me but from runners like Pre and Kenny and Jack and George Bowman back at Mount Hermon Academy in the Berkshire Mountains of western Massachusetts; from every honest athlete who knew the searing pain of that penultimate 800-meter interval and honorably shared the burden of setting the pace.

Juicing made a mockery out of that pain and sacrifice. Just as my father had robbed me and my siblings of our childhoods, the state-sponsored East German doping system had cheated honest athletes out of the striving that gave our lives meaning. I knew what it was like to win honestly, to fight it out with yourself. As was the case with my father, I was powerless to declare the truth. I had no proof of any crime, and even if I did have proof, the criminals could twist and obfuscate it. Out in the world, no one would have a reason or incentive to countenance my story.

On the plus side of the ledger, I was proud of making it through the marathon while dealing with my foot injury. In Munich I had shown that I could run well when everything was falling my way; in Montreal I had proved that I could run well when the gods frowned on me. I was 28 years old and still in my prime.

Meanwhile, the paradigm was shifting, both for ill and for good. This dark thing, this shadow of cheating, had infiltrated the sport, but it was now becoming feasible to earn a living as a professional runner. And part of being a professional—maybe the heart of the vocation—was learning how to lose. No matter how thoroughly you plan and think and train, no matter how much pain you're willing to absorb—and even for the cheaters, no matter how diabolically powerful your drugs—you are always, ineluctably, going to lose more than you win.

I knew that many superb athletes derived their energy and ascribed their success to a visceral hatred of losing. As I drove away from the Montreal Olympics, I kept thinking that there might be another way.

✦ ✦ ✦

I started to reframe as soon as I drove out of Montreal. I remained in a state of stunned disbelief. I wasn't angry and wasn't even frustrated in the normal sense of the term, even though I knew right away, knew in my bones, that we'd been deceived. And it wasn't just me—every honest runner in the field had been played for a sucker. Don Kardong, for instance, who'd belted his guts out, ran a smart, hard-closing race, only to finish a heartbreaking bridesmaid's fourth. Don deserved a bronze medal. I already had a gold medal from Munich, and I'd just added a silver. What if Don never got this close to a medal again?

Still, I wasn't angry. Anger wouldn't do any good. I thought back over the race, from the semi-comic disaster of my racing flats falling apart to the vision of Bruce McDonald flinging the back-up pair of shoes over the fence—the shoes turning against the gray sky like a satellite spinning in orbit—to the raindrops spattering the inside lane of the Tartan track to the early miles in which I played hide-and-seek with Lasse Viren, to the point where I made my break on Mount Royal and Cierpinski appeared as if he'd parachuted in or stepped off the sidewalk like the imposter at the Munich Marathon.

And on through the miles when I trailed Cierpinski, vainly waiting for him to flame out. And finally, as I drove south through the warm humid night back across the border into the States, an indelible image seemed to fill the windshield: Cierpinski at the 23-mile mark, after I'd worked his lead down to that manageable thread. He had looked back over his shoulder, met my eyes, and then turned and soared away.

There was nothing I would have done differently. I had performed honorably. Once I got dropped, I had not quit. I drew everything out of myself that I possibly could. I hadn't committed any tactical errors. I hadn't been like Pre in the 5000 in Munich, when he'd lost his head and run all of the final lap in lane 2, adding extra meters to his race and causing him to finish fourth instead of among the top three—the mistake drove Bowerman crazy. Now Pre was gone and would never win the medal he deserved, while Waldemar Cierpinski, prior to 1976 an average, national-class steeplechaser, was the Olympic Marathon champion.

I had done everything within my power, but I hadn't rung up the gold medal that America expected. By this time, however, the nation had moved on. The American running scene was no longer a small enterprise that relied on charismatic leaders or personalities; it had matured into a grassroots way of life for hundreds of thousands of people, including a dynamic, creative core of leaders who were organizing road races and founding running clubs around the nation.

There was nothing marketed or manufactured about any of this. The movement was growing organically and changing lives for the better, and this side of the sport, this swelling citizen's road racing side, grew in tandem with the shadow blighting its elite dimension. I wasn't about to dial down my competitive career at this point, but as I drove away from Montreal, as I departed the scene of yet another crime that I couldn't talk about, I sensed that a page had turned and that my future would increasingly lie with the bright, hopeful side of the sport.

18

Father of the Boom

Early in the autumn after the Games, I ran in the first five-borough New York City Marathon, which in my opinion, more than my Munich victory, marked the true start of the running boom. Prior to '76, the New York City Marathon had been run entirely within Central Park, a significant logistical feat in itself. Expanding the race to encompass the entire city, engaging each borough, lifted the marathon to another level.

Again, the idea wasn't machine-generated by the Chamber of Commerce or a marketing firm: It grew out of the brain of a man named Fred Lebow and the friends he ran with in the city—accomplished men such as George Hirsch and Allan Steinfeld. But the vision and energy came mostly from Lebow, whose drive, salesmanship, and brains could have made him a prince of the city in whatever field he chose. Fred chose running; specifically, he chose the marathon. Fred Lebow epitomized the type of leader that was energizing running communities in almost every major American city.

The aura of the '76 New York City Marathon was similar to the vibe that had emanated out of Hayward Field back at the '72 Olympic Marathon Trials, but this was bigger, brighter, and even more inclusive. New York proved that the marathon was possible for anybody. At that point the tent wasn't as wide as it's grown today—only serious competitive runners attempted the distance, and meeting a time, not merely finishing, was the goal for most athletes—but the five-borough parade, the civic celebration, the spontaneous street party, the river of runners of all description irrevocably led to the democratization of the marathon. I welcomed this development. While I always respected the marathon and acknowledged its singular set of demands and rewards, I always thought it was a mountain that, with sufficient thought and effort, virtually anyone could climb.

Indeed, in 1976, despite Cierpinski's Olympic gold medal, the marathon remained an American-dominated enterprise, with scores of US men, the vast majority of them citizen-athletes, capable of running 2:20 or better. Bill Rodgers and I temporarily occupied the peak of this pyramid, and as the race wound through the city, he and I battled for the lead. By now Bill had recovered from his hamstring injury, while I was continuing to deal with my defining foot and ankle problem. I ran a solid 2:13:12 but finished a distant second to Bill, who ran 2:10:10. His victory helped cement his identity as a master of America's name-brand marathons, as he strung together a chain of triumphs in both New York City and Boston. After that race people anticipated a long glorious rivalry building between the two of us. We were both the same age but at different stages of our respective careers. Bill's arc was on the rise. I still had a lot of good races in front of me, but I had already logged my signature performances.

Rodgers and I met again at the Boston Marathon in April 1977. It was my first Boston. I had never quite bonded with the legendary Boston Marathon and its Boston Athletic Association (BAA) organizers, led in those days by Jock Semple. You might think that with my fondness for tradition and decorum, I would have loved the Boston Marathon, which was steeped in those qualities. But instead I found the BAA to be hidebound and self-righteous in its approach, almost as arrogant as Avery Brundage and the US Olympic Committee (UIC) were.

A few years before, I had approached the BAA, said I wanted to run Boston, and all I asked for was a plane ticket because airfare was expensive from Florida. Jock Semple said no; he wouldn't budge, which reminded me of the first reaction of that medical school dean in New Mexico—when instead of giving a good reason for not accommodating my request, all she could say was "because I did it this way."

But by 1977 I had patched up my differences with Semple. I traveled to Boston on Patriots' Day for another round with the hometown hero, "Boston Billy" Rodgers. I had spent the winter training in Boulder, following my tried-and-true system, although now, nursing my ankle injury, I couldn't run the hard days quite as hard or log my intervals quite as fast. Now in Boston we took the bus out to Hopkinton, and I started fast as usual; in fact, even faster than usual because that first mile out of the village plunges sharply downhill. The whole first half of the course follows a downhill trajectory, and if the wind is at your back, you can book indeed. We went through the half in a very fast 1:04, a world-record pace.

But then it happened—the dime finally dropped on my lower-leg injury. My foot blew up, not quite severely enough to drive me out of the race but enough to knock me far off the lead. The scenario of our Olympic Marathon Trials was reversed. Bill Rodgers powered away to his second consecutive Boston victory, while I limped across the line far out of contention, in 2:18. The day after the marathon I flew straight to Eugene, where Dr. Stan James, the preeminent sports orthopedist in the nation, hung his shingle.

During surgery, Dr. James found that a tendon had pulled away part of my navicular bone. He repaired the break, but this was the defining injury that is every honest runner's lot.

+ + +

Running remained my passion, but now the sport was also my profession, forming the base for a range of business interests. The running boom had opened the door to speaking engagements, broadcasting commentary, and the like. But frustratingly, absurdly, a competitive runner still couldn't directly make an aboveboard living from the sport. Due to the strictures of the Olympics, the tail wagging the track-and-field dog, an increasingly untenable amateurism stubbornly held sway in the sport. Meet promoters and shoe company executives could pay you under the table, but in order to maintain your Olympic eligibility, you couldn't earn money in the light of day.

But the pressure was building. Road racing was growing more popular around the nation and the world, and new talent was flooding into the sport. Why shouldn't professional runners get paid like pro relief pitchers or free safeties? The governing body tried to adapt. The Amateur Athletic Union (AAU) evolved into an entity called the Athletics Congress, or TAC, which came up with a batch of convoluted rules in a clumsy attempt to bring the sport into the modern era.

For instance, under the old AAU system, a runner couldn't sell his name to a running-shoe store, deriving income from the name and career he had developed. TAC slightly softened that position. For instance, I convinced Ollan Cassell that I could put my name on a store and have it not be considered an endorsement if I owned the store, capitalized it, was on the bank loan guarantees, and worked there. By the same token, you couldn't get paid outright for endorsing a product in the way, for example, that US marathoner Meb Keflezighi would get paid for endorsing Skechers or Epson in the 21st century. In 1976 a runner's photo or likeness could not appear in an ad unless said athlete was an employee of the company she or he was representing.

It all seemed silly and self-defeating. Elite runners couldn't make a living, and American teams couldn't compete with athletes whose nations supported their full-time commitment to their sport. I decided to give the wheel a shove, in the way that Pre had shoved it with the nonsanctioned track meet with the Finns back in 1975. Hilton, the international hotel chain, wanted to retool its properties to attract guests who were less interested in loading up at the prime-rib and cheesecake buffet tables than they were in working out at the gym and running on trails. Hilton was looking for a personality to sell its new fitness plan, and who better to do so than the 1972 gold medal winner in the marathon, the media-proclaimed father of the running boom?

That would have been verboten under the old order. But David Geyer, a West Coast–based ad executive, runner, and friend of George Hirsch, engineered a three-way deal among Hilton Hotels, TAC, and me. Under the arrangement, Hilton paid a fee to TAC, which agreed to supply an amateur athlete (in this case, yours truly) to appear in a commercial for the company. Hilton contracted with me as a consultant to design several running routes around their hotels and suggest healthy options for their restaurant menus. I presented the deal to Ollan Cassell, the head of TAC. Ollan and I had a connection through Bob Giegengack. As coach of 1964 US Olympic track team, Geig had placed a slightly injured Cassell into the gold-medal-winning 4 × 400 relay team. Ollan agreed to the Hilton deal, and we filmed the commercial at the Waldorf Astoria in New York City.

A few years later, a group of US distance runners raised a more direct challenge to the system. Organizers of the popular Cascade Run Off road race in Portland, Oregon, offered to openly pay appearance and prize money to a number of invited elite athletes. That would have been in direct violation of TAC rules and would have forced the hand of the officials. I knew that such a development was inevitable—runners would have to start getting paid sooner or later. The sport couldn't mature, and American athletes couldn't compete equally on the international stage without a more realistic financial framework. However, I thought a confrontation was unnecessary. Again, due to my standing in the sport and my personal relationships and legal training, I helped broker a compromise.

Huddling with Bob Stone, the attorney I worked for and ran with and who had helped structure the deal with Hilton, and Steve Bosley, a banker in Boulder who helped finance my business projects and with whom I'd founded the Bolder Boulder 10-K, we came up with a plan. We called it the TAC Trust, a system by which athletes could earn prize money and appearance and endorsement fees. They could use a portion of that money to directly support their training and living expenses, with the remainder, if there was any, to be held in trust for use after the athlete retired from competition.

Cassell was instrumental in selling the idea to the International Association of Athletics Federations (IAAF), which at the time was looking for a solution to the problem of Eastern Bloc countries lavishly financing and rewarding their "amateur" athletes, under the pretext that their support came from the government, as part of their communal system. Fortunately, there were more IAAF voters from the West than from the Eastern Bloc, and the governing body agreed to the TAC Trust concept.

That arrangement mollified the IAAF and the International Olympic Committee (IOC), which continued to grant TAC Trust runners amateur status and subsequent eligibility for the Olympics. Although it may seem unwieldy now, the TAC Trust system formed a serviceable bridge to a more comprehensive professionalism, which followed incrementally over the next few years. By 1992, the Olympic Games were open to professional athletes in all sports. That development created a new batch of problems, but the net result was clearly positive; the system's former hypocrisy and inefficiency no longer prevailed.

Meanwhile, I pursued other opportunities. With Steve Bosley serving as my banker, I opened the first running specialty store in Boulder, one of the first stores of its kind in the United States. From the jump, I envisioned the store as a nexus for the running community as much as a place to buy and sell shoes and apparel. We hired young, competitive runners to serve as salesclerks, providing them with a source of income along with flexible hours that encouraged their training and racing. Mary Decker and Herb Lindsay clocked hours at the store, which first occupied a pocket-sized space at the back of a building but soon moved to a larger space on the Pearl Street Mall.

We started a clothing line, Frank Shorter Sports, producing and marketing running apparel. We were the first company to use Gore-Tex in running gear and the first firm to stitch key pockets into running shorts. Both the store and the clothing line were profitable. I wasn't involved in the businesses full-time, although I went to the store, the company offices, or both nearly every business day when I was in town. I was still training full bore, competing in road races and track meets and providing color commentary for telecasts of running events. I was lucky to have great people managing the businesses, several of whom went on to successful careers in the industry. I liquidated the store in the mid-1980s as part of the settlement in my divorce from Louise. The clothing line has survived through several iterations and changes of ownership, and it continues to be a popular brand in Europe.

Through the late 1970s I maintained my position among the top-ranked marathoners and 10,000-meter runners in the world. But the world was catching up with me and other American runners. Ironically, the increased competition sprang directly from our efforts to professionalize the sport. Athletes from East Africa were getting scholarships to American colleges, and others competed for prize money in the growing number of US road races. Meanwhile, buoyed by the brazen success of Cierpinski and other suspected juicers, and emboldened by the fact that the sport's governing body either looked the other way or proved totally incapable of testing and policing for performance-enhancing drugs, European distance runners vied with the Africans for the top places at big meets and road races.

At the same time, the politicization of international sports in general, and the Olympics in particular, deepened. After 1976, when some key African nations boycotted the Montreal Games, a similar scenario took shape for the 1980 Olympic Games in Moscow. To protest the Soviet invasion of Afghanistan, the United States threatened to lead the Western nations in a boycott. That movement further darkened the prospects of a rising generation of elite American runners, who already had to cope with increased competition from Africa and Europe. At the '80 US Marathon Olympic Trials, talents such as Bill Rodgers, Craig Virgin, and Alberto Salazar were either emerging or hitting their peak. Their dreams of Olympic medals, however, vanished down a black geopolitical hole: Shortly after the trials concluded, President Jimmy Carter confirmed the American-led boycott of the Moscow Olympics.

So even if I had still been at or near the top of my game, I wouldn't have had another shot at an Olympic Marathon medal. But I was well beyond my peak by that point. I did compete in the '80 Olympic Marathon Trials, but slowed by injury and the accumulation of years (by then I was 33), I only managed a 2:24 performance, finishing far out of contention. So what happened at the shadowed Moscow Games? By the logic of honest distance running, Waldemar Cierpinski shouldn't have been a contender; following the pattern of Lasse Viren, in the years following the 1976 Olympics, Cierpinski faded into an average performer at best on the international scene. But in Moscow, lo and behold, Cierpinski reappeared in all the glory he had demonstrated in Montreal, masterfully blasting away from the field, winning a second consecutive gold medal in the marathon, becoming a national hero in East Germany, and staking a claim as the equal of authentic iconic Olympians such as Bikila and Zátopek.

Just as my father didn't bother watching my gold medal run in Munich in '72, I passed on watching Cierpinski's marathon in Moscow. Also similar to the case of my father, and the Black September killers, I didn't honor the East German with a single thought. People assumed that I bore an animus toward Cierpinski, but that wasn't the case. I coped by focusing on matters within my control and sphere of influence. In Boulder I continued to work out twice a day, at 11:30 a.m. and 3:30 p.m. if my schedule permitted, extending my lifelong experiment in self-coaching, my attempt to lay down a bedrock consistency. Now, however, I ran for the same purpose as during my early years at Yale: as a way to relieve stress and set up the rest of my busy day.

Increasingly, speaking engagements filled my schedule. All sorts of audiences asked me to explain the nature and allure of distance running in general, and the marathon in particular. "It's like reading a good book," I told one group. "After a while you're not really conscious of reading. It's just images racing through your head. It's the same with running the marathon. People always ask me why I do it. Well, I'm good at it, and we do the things we excel at. But also, I just like being out there. I like it better than anything else I've ever done. I like being able to think about it as I go along. I get so seriously involved with the race, with what my body is doing, I don't have time to notice things around me."

As the years and decades unreeled, as one Olympiad followed another, as the citizen-running movement continued to swell and elite American distance running continued to decline, as one doping scandal gave rise to the next one, my story, my explanation, didn't really change. Amid the corruption and cynicism and politics, and the failure of shoe companies or other entities to manufacture an American running icon who approached the stature of a Steve Prefontaine, my star seemed to burn steadily through the years. On the women's side, Joan Benoit achieved a brilliant career, culminating with her gold medal in the marathon at the 1984 Olympics in Los Angeles. But since 1972, no American man has won an Olympic gold medal in a race longer than 400 meters.

That left me in rarefied but lonely air. It seemed as if my marathon had never really ended and that my ghosts had never quite stopped chasing me—or perhaps I had never ceased pursuing them.

19

The House on Wisner Avenue

It was a December morning in 2010, and winter had struck the Rockies. Dark clouds boiled over the Flatirons, and an icy wind scoured down from the mountains over the western edge of the Great Plains. I was in my house in Boulder, on the bank of Wonderland Lake. I stood in my kitchen with a mug of coffee, watching the runners work the trail around the water.

I had bought this house in 2000 after my divorce from Paddy, my second wife. Our daughter, Julie, grew up here; now she was in veterinary school at Colorado State University in Fort Collins. She has two older brothers: Alex, a mechanical engineer on the faculty at the University of Michigan, and Mark, a law school graduate out in California.

Paddy and I divorced, after 15 years of marriage. My first marriage, to Louise, the boys' mother, had also lasted 15 years. You might think the divorces had stemmed from issues pertaining to my troubled childhood—matters of trust and intimacy, problems that had plagued the relationships of many of my siblings. But I can't attribute my failed unions to the physical and psychological violence of my father. My own actions had caused the end of my first marriage, and a combination of factors brought on divorce number two.

I sipped coffee and waved through the wide back window to a young mother pushing a jogging stroller. The young mom waved back at the skinny, silver-haired gent standing in his warm kitchen in his workout clothes. I was 64 years old, and a few weeks earlier my first grandchild had been born. Would that young mom know she was waving to the media-proclaimed father of the running boom? Not likely.

The woman was a member of the new running tribe, one much larger than the original movement of the 1970s. Today's runners were predominately female and mostly unconcerned with time or performance. They were more focused on fitness, personal growth, and on raising money for various good causes. In their running lives, they evidenced little of the obsession that characterized my time but also less of the fire. That was fine by me. During my talks at running events around the country, I worked hard at relating to this new audience. I believed in broadening the tent and welcoming everybody. I was continuing my career-long campaign to demystify the marathon and open the distance up to runners like that pretty young mom rounding a bend on the trail and disappearing out of sight.

A moment later two boomer runners appeared, wearing knee supports and fleece vests, moving at about a 10-minute-mile pace, which was what I managed nowadays. A year earlier I had undergone hip-resurfacing surgery. I was also managing a degenerative disc problem in my back. Although I still worked out twice a day, at 11:30 a.m. and 3:30 p.m. if at all possible, I had to ration my running mileage. That was all right, too. I accepted the inevitability of aging. My goal now was to slow down as gracefully as possible. I rarely raced anymore. In the year ahead, however, there was one event I did not intend to miss: Middletown's Classic 10-K in June. Other key events on my calendar included the Bolder Boulder 10-K, the Indy Mini in Indianapolis, the Bass Pro Shop Fitness Festival in Springfield, Missouri, and the Falmouth Road Race in Cape Cod.

Out on the lakeside trail, the older runners had caught sight of me and were waving excitedly. I had evolved into something of a boomer icon and a local institution. Steve Bosley had commissioned a life-size bronze statue of me that stood by the Bolder Boulder course in the middle of the University of Colorado campus.

The phone rang, and I jumped, the sound preternaturally loud in the empty, high-ceilinged house. I picked up the receiver. "Hello, Mac McAvoy from the Fort Wayne Track Club in Indiana calling for Frank Shorter, please." The voice was tight, a little nervous, a guy making a cold call.

"This is Frank," I replied. There was a surprised silence on the line—Frank Shorter answering his own phone? But that's how I had always played it, ever since watching Mark Spitz back at Munich and vowing to handle myself differently. No entourage, no agent, and during most stages of my career not even an office assistant to field my telephone calls.

Mac from Fort Wayne made his pitch: Come to town in January to deliver the keynote speech at the annual meeting of the track club. And while you're here for the weekend, go out for a fun run with the board members, rub elbows with the rank and file, give some media interviews, and so on. "I think you'll like Fort Wayne, Frank," Mac said. "We had Bill Rodgers come out for the weekend last year."

I flipped through my calendar for January: an appearance at a 10-K in Florida; a panel discussion at a marathon in New Orleans. The Fort Wayne weekend looked open. I accepted the offer.

"That's just great!" Mac said. "We'll put you up in a nice hotel."

I said thanks, but I'd prefer to stay in the home of one of the local runners. Mac said sure; that could be arranged.

I hung up, refilled my mug with coffee, and returned to the window. I considered the work I'd have to put in to gracefully complete that fun run in Fort Wayne in January. At my age and in my condition, I had to think about every mile. After Fort Wayne, there would be plenty of time to recover and prepare for Middletown. I went back to my hometown road race almost every year, starting with the first edition in 1981. In that race I had battled Bill Rodgers in a contest that some people in town still remembered.

Back in '81, Bill was hitting his prime, and I was on a long, gradual downward competitive arc. But I wasn't going to let anyone beat me on my hometown turf, especially Bill Rodgers. We had broken away from the pack at the gun and had run in each other's pocket the rest of the way. About a mile from the finish line at the Orange County fairgrounds, Rodgers had started one of his long, grinding dogged surges. Digging deep, however, I was able to hang with him. Over the last quarter mile, heading into the finish, I had launched my own surge, pulling away from Rodgers to win by nine seconds.

A national running magazine had published a feature story on the race, which had been among my final top-shelf performances. I had a copy of the magazine somewhere around the house, buried deep in my files.

The Middletown 10-K. I loved going back every year, during

the first weekend in June. I would give a little welcoming talk at the starting line and visit with old friends, whose number dwindled each year. Most of the people I grew up with had left the town. The YMCA was still going strong in the old Clemson mansion, but our old house, the one with the mansard roof, wraparound porch, and separate ground floor entrance, had fallen into disrepair. The last time I had driven past, a few years before, the place appeared vacant, and a for-sale sign jutted crookedly in the weedy front yard.

So, no, there weren't many old friends left for me to look up, and, of course, I never went to visit my father, who had retired in the town, living with his second wife in a house not far from the high school stadium and the 10-K finishing line. He was still esteemed in Middletown. Rumors sometimes circulated, people whispering that the doc, like many dads back in the 1950s and '60s, had sometimes leaned a little too hard into the spanking and other "corporal punishment." But nobody in town knew the truth—or wanted to know it. Every year I returned for the race a little grayer, a little slower. And every year I would feel my father's presence, a dark, malevolent force field that was almost palpable, driving me away from his house. I stayed away until 2008, just before I went in for the hip surgery, the June that Dr. Sam was dying.

After that macabre Olympic-medal celebration in Middletown in 1972, I did not see my father more than a half-dozen times over the next 40 years. I never allowed my three children—his grandchildren—to be alone with him. That became clear on a visit to Boulder that I permitted when Alex, our firstborn, was still very young.

Dr. Sam came to stay with our family, and each morning he would go to pick the paper off the front porch. One morning

Smokey, our family's pet dachshund, escaped out the door when my father reached for the paper. Grumbling, he had to go out in his bathrobe and retrieve the animal. The next morning the scene replayed. Smokey again tried to bolt when my father opened the door to fetch the paper. But this time he savagely slammed the door on the dog as it crossed the doorsill. Smokey howled; our baby cried. I took the dog to the vet for treatment for broken ribs.

After that episode, I never permitted another lengthy visit from my father. I kept no photographs of him, either on the shelves or in a scrapbook or in storage. Interestingly, as the kids got older, they never asked about their grandfather. I just told the children that it was better not to see him. The kids sensed that something was deeply wrong with the man, and with the instinctive wisdom of children, they did not pursue the matter.

I stuffed my father back into an emotional box, but then, like a ghost from Dickens's *A Christmas Carol,* he popped back up at a road race in Florida in 1991. I was then about a decade removed from my pro-level running career. My Olympic Marathon Trials in 1980 had pretty much put a lid on my world-class ambitions and sealed the number of national titles I'd won at 24. But I was still actively involved in the running scene, perhaps even more involved than when I was world-ranked. I managed the clothing line, worked frequently as a commentator for NBC, spoke at race and marathon expos, gave frequent media interviews, and generally served as an ambassador for the sport.

In that latter capacity I appeared at the 10-K in Fort Lauderdale. The race benefited a local center for abused and battered children, and a reporter from the local newspaper approached me for an interview. Perhaps she struck a particularly sympathetic tone, maybe I was affected by meeting the kids at the center, or perhaps my emotional fist simply unclenched in the warm Florida sunshine—but something got me talking.

I told the reporter that, when I was a child, my father had abused me but provided no details. At that stage of my life, I still repressed the memories of specific incidents. Instead of details such as the Felix the Cat tattoo, I just recalled a single undifferentiated mass of violence. It was like that moment at the military hospital in Munich, when I tried to imagine my parents at the time of my birth and could only picture two amorphous, barely sentient beings.

So I supplied no proof to back my claim. Also, in that pre-Internet, pre-social media, pre-priest-abuse-exposure age, awareness of the issue wasn't a fraction of what it is today. I lacked the context and vocabulary—in distance-running parlance, I lacked the base—to engage the matter with authority and insight. And finally, and most urgently, in 1991 my father was still very much alive. Dr. Sam was living back in Middletown with his second wife, still a hero to the town, still living his double life, and I still feared the man.

My reticence sprang from yet another source. I recoiled from joining the therapeutic age. I refused to become one of those aging rock stars or politicians clamoring for attention or votes by whining about their unhappy childhoods. I felt no need to aggrandize myself or serve as talk-show fodder. Ever since Munich, I had tried to present a public face of probity and a certain dignity—at bottom I still sought to be that Yale gentleman molded by Coach Giegengack.

The reporter wrote her story. Despite its thinness, it drew notice; in abridged version, it was reprinted in the *New York Times*. But since my father denied any wrongdoing and I couldn't or wouldn't provide corroborating evidence or details, the story soon died. To tell the truth, I was more relieved than disappointed. My late stab at justice had been uncharacteristically clumsy. It had been ill-timed and poorly aimed. Maybe it was better—certainly, it was easier—to let my father's crimes stay buried.

I went back to my life of denial in Boulder, and Dr. Sam returned to his life of denial in Middletown. In their homes scattered across the country, my sisters and brothers continued to writhe with their private, unresolved pain. I got busy again, always moving ahead, because as long as I was moving, I didn't have to give my father a thought.

I brooded on these matters in my kitchen in Boulder, on that early-winter morning in 2010. My coffee had gone cold. E-mail messages had piled up on my computer monitor, most of them having to do with the US Anti-Doping Agency (USADA) and doping, but I didn't have the heart to open them. It was time to go to the gym for my late-morning workout, normally a chore I relished, but today I didn't want to go. Thoughts of my father, usually repressed or else spontaneously bobbing up in isolated floes, crashed down that morning like ice from a calving glacier.

The final time I saw him had been in Middletown in June 2008, when I had traveled back for the 10-K. My father, age 86, was dying from kidney failure. My sister Amie had relayed the news. Dr. Sam was under hospice care in his house on Wisner Avenue, just a block away from the high school and the start and finish of the 10-K course. He had only a week or less to live—the very same week of the Middletown road race, when his son always came back to snub the old man, making quite clear, at least to the two of them, that the son had established a good life free of his father's evil control.

On the plane ride east from Denver, I considered the situation with a bitter smile. Dr. Sam and his monstrous ego, his twisted sense of theater, and his bottomless hunger for attention: Even for his death he chose a time of high drama and maximum inconvenience for the people close to him—or, that is, the people who should have been close to him.

Should I give in and pay a visit to the dying man? In Middletown, on the Saturday before the race, I went back and forth on the question. For the past few years, on each of my visits to Middletown, I had stayed at the home of Valerie Kilcoin and her husband, Bill, the same Valerie who, as a schoolgirl, had secretly watched me run by her house and thought, what a dreamboat, the boy with the perfect life. Now, over a late-afternoon drink, Valerie and I would laugh about those days. I had never told her the truth about my life at the house on Highland Avenue. And now, in 2008, I did not tell Valerie that my father was dying.

I went about my rounds on that bright, warm, prerace Saturday. I visited Frank Giannino, the race organizer, at his specialty running store on the highway leading out of town. I sat down for an interview with Kevin Gleason, the sports editor of the local *Times Herald-Record*. Frank and Kevin had followed my career for years. They had heard the intimations and rumors about my father. Like most Middletowners, Frank simply could not wrap his head around the possibility that the beloved physician—the doc who'd made house calls when Frank was a kid—was in fact a secret monster. Frank allowed that the man might have been strict, inflicting corporal punishment that may have drawn close to the line, but certainly he hadn't crossed the line. And certainly you couldn't judge a father of the benighted 1950s by the more enlightened standards of the 21st century.

Kevin Gleason, for his part, was more skeptical about my father's reputation and open to the possibility that he was capable of violence against his children. In fact, a few years earlier, Kevin had written a story for the paper that revisited the claims I had made at the race in Florida in the 1990s. Readers had reacted angrily to Kevin's article; like Frank Giannino they could not countenance the prospect of the doctor criminally abusing his own children. Now, in our 2008 interview, Kevin did not ask about my father, but he left openings in the conversation, doors I might have walked through had I wanted to. Several times during the interview, I had reached for the knob but could not quite bring myself to turn it.

But finally, late in the day, I felt the house on Wisner Avenue pulling at me. It pulled with a magnetic force as irresistible as the power that had driven me away from the house all the previous years. What the hell, I thought. What did I have to lose? What more did I have to fear?

In the early evening before the race, I went to visit my father. I didn't expect anything. I didn't want anything. But there I was ringing the doorbell at the house on a quiet street by the high school. A female hospice attendant let me in and led me back to the room where my father lay on a hospital bed. I had interrupted his sponge bath. He was totally nude, heavily sedated but not comatose. The attendant continued to bathe him. She talked to me about him as if he wasn't there or couldn't understand what she was saying. But one look in his eye and I could tell he was furious about his helpless state. It was the same look as when he would grab my arm to beat me.

The woman turned and asked if I wanted some time alone with my father but I said no, that's all right. In fact, I felt better having her there. For protection? For a semblance of normalcy? A bulwark against an embarrassing spontaneous outpouring of emotion? I hardly expected any manner of reconciliation, but I think I was looking for a gesture, some chink of acknowledgment that could lead to what . . . forgiveness? I didn't think so. I didn't know. I just felt as if I had to see my dying father and finally catch a glimpse of the true man behind all his masks and playacting.

And there he was, naked and helpless and vulnerable. You might think that I would feel a faint stab of pity for a human being in the situation that sooner or later was every soul's fate. But I didn't feel pity. What I felt, staring into those clouded eyes, was an enormous sense of relief. Now he couldn't hurt me anymore. He couldn't hurt my mother (who died two years later, in 2010); he couldn't hurt my sisters or brothers. He couldn't hurt anyone.

I left the house and went out into the warm June twilight, savoring the eastern humidity and fecundity after being so long in the dry West. I breathed deeply and felt a bolt of liberation, similar to how I had felt as a boy when I used to break free from the house on Highland Avenue to run up to the park and stop at the home of the Prestons, normal functional people who cared for their loved ones instead of afflicting them.

The next day I stepped to the starting line of the 10-K. I said a few words, recalling how I had run these same streets when I was a boy. I explained that I still ran with a left-leaning hitch in my stride because I had carried my books in my left arm when I ran to school in the morning.

The gun sounded, and we set out through the quiet Sunday morning streets. The old boys in front of the firehouse waved to me, hollering "Way to go, Frank, welcome home Frank!" And I waved back, and I waved to the children and their parents on the sidewalk. Then I ran into the stadium across the finish line. Later that day I flew home to Colorado, and when I landed at the airport in Denver, there was a message on my phone from my sister Amie saying our father had died while I was in-flight. It was really over now. I did not return to Middletown for the funeral.

At last, it seemed I was truly free from my father. I waited for a lasting sense of release, a lightening like the one I had briefly but intensely felt as I left the house on that June evening. Perhaps at my age, my station in life, it was foolish to expect such a breakthrough. Maybe the very idea of it—a concept that seemed related to "closure"—was no more than a construct of the talk-show culture that I was so determined to avoid.

I went about my work, my life, which remained full. I had my children. Despite the orthopedic tax payments that had come due on all those thousands of hard miles and a bout with skin cancer, I enjoyed good health. I was still in demand on the running circuit. In fact, I might have been more popular than ever. Although I resisted the label, people regarded me as a throwback figure. Along with Bill Rodgers and Joan Benoit Samuelson, I was one of the triumvirate of the golden age of American marathoners. We had made our marks and established our legacies before the sport evolved into a marketed and managed product, before the East Africans established their elite-level dominance, and before the corrosions of doping. We had earned our reputations when running was still fresh and new, a tool of personal and social transformation, a way of knowing, a path to self-knowledge and transcendence, and a way to build authentic community—a Tao.

Not that present-day runners couldn't develop and discover these same qualities, and not that I hadn't capitalized on the opportunities that the business side of the sport afforded me. Lord knows, I was no ascetic and certainly no saint. There were still pure, saintlike runners out there—I recalled the hippie dishwasher who used to pound tempo runs with the lawyers and me back in the 1970s—but they didn't live in high-ceilinged, sun-filled houses on the edge of Wonderland Lake in the shadow of the Flatirons. They weren't invited to fly around the nation and the world. I had recently returned from a USO-organized trip to run with military members serving in Iraq, for instance.

Yes, I counted myself lucky to be going full speed into my 60s and still engaged in the scene. Most prominently, over the last decade, I had assumed a leadership role in the anti-doping movement. People assumed my bond to the issue formed back in 1976 in Montreal, when Waldemar Cierpinski had looked back over his shoulder at me at the 21-mile mark and then surged away. But, in fact, my active involvement in the campaign began decades later, the result of a run that I took with President Bill Clinton.

20

The Oval Office

The run was arranged by Billy Webster, assistant White House chief of staff, who was an avid runner and a friend of George Hirsch. President Clinton was then in the third year of his first term, a youngish man who often finished his runs at a McDonald's restaurant not far from the White House, where he would schmooze with the patrons. By that time running had evolved into a virtual boilerplate photo op for US presidents and other political leaders, an ideal vehicle for appearing vigorous, health-conscious, and youth-friendly.

President Clinton would undoubtedly have preferred to run with a current American distance star, a young woman or man who had won or at least contended at the New York or Boston or Olympic marathons, but no Americans of this caliber were available. Elite US distance running was in near total eclipse. East Africans and North Africans dominated. Americans didn't even try to compete with them. From the 800 meters on up, there were no Americans anywhere near the annual top-10 world-best lists. More than a decade had passed since Joan Benoit had won her gold medal at the 1984 Los Angeles Olympics and 13 years since Alberto Salazar and Dick Beardsley had battled at the Duel in the Sun at the 1982 Boston Marathon. Despite the growth of the sport on the citizen-runner level and the rapid increase in the number of marathons, no runner approaching the level of a Steve Prefontaine had emerged to galvanize American sports fans. Unfortunately, the most recognizable names in the sport were still us aging rock stars. Thus the call from the president's office.

Bill and I met President Clinton in the pre-dawn darkness, and we rode in a limousine to a park along the Potomac that had been cordoned off for the President's morning run. I knew Mr. Clinton was an experienced runner; I had met him years earlier at a 4th of July 5-K in Little Rock, when he was governor of Arkansas. And now he showed that he was quite fit. We covered the three miles in a very respectable 24 minutes, conversing the whole time.

And after the run, instead of shaking hands and saying adios, President Clinton invited Bill and me into the presidential limousine, where we sat cheek by jowl with the Secret Service agents in their shades. In fact, one of the agents had run with us, keeping a few strides behind the leader of the Western World, causing me to flash briefly on the Munich Massacre and Marathon. We climbed into the limo with the president, and instead of going to McDonald's, we drove back to the White House. We hung out for a half hour discussing all manner of subjects; then the president showed us the Oval Office. That made me recall Leningrad in 1970, my first big international race, when I had looked at the Soviet runner and thought, yes, I'm really here; I'm in Russia. Now I thought, yes, I'm really here; I'm in the Oval Office.

Finally, Rodgers and I shook hands with the chief executive and took our leave. I was impressed by the president and grateful for the experience, but I thought that was the end of it. The moment constituted yet another perk of winning that Munich gold medal, one more golden memory. My run with President Clinton sank back beneath the press of life but resurfaced in a totally unexpected way in 1998.

+ + +

The late 1990s. I was busy with family, business, travel, training, racing, public speaking, commentating for NBC because Dick Ebersol, then sports director for the network, was an old Yale classmate—yet another Bulldog connection. On the air I took pains to provide quiet, meaningful insights rather than thump-the-tub clichés, such as the notoriously bonehead post-competition question hurled at an athlete when she's still trying to catch her breath: What were you thinking when Gloria made her move? Although, everybody knows that in the heat of competition, properly speaking, the accomplished athlete wasn't really thinking at all.

Plus, I had my cancer scare in 1995, when a seemingly harmless pimple at the corner of my lip bloomed into a dangerous skin cancer, perhaps the product of all those miles I had run under the baking sun in Colorado, New Mexico, and Florida. The oncologist told me we had to get the growth out right away. Less than a week passed between diagnosis and removal, which turned out to be an hours-long ordeal requiring major reconstructive plastic surgery. It turned out fine, and the dermatologist got all of the tumor before it had metastasized.

In a word, life was happening, and while it did, the elite running world spun to a tune keyed to performance-enhancing drugs. That was obvious, given the absurdly fast times being logged. Since the sport's inception, world records had crept down incrementally, by fractions of a second, recorded by seasoned performers who had perfected their crafts over years of exacting study and labor. But now suddenly, inexperienced runners were chopping minutes off record times. Watching these blazingly fast races, you noticed that the leaders simply didn't get tired. The essence of endurance running was fatigue—dealing with it, fighting it, and embracing it— but these guys didn't get tired. By the same token, in baseball it had always been very difficult to belt a home run, and suddenly light-hitting shortstops were slamming 50 homers a season. But somehow the average fan, the average sportswriter, just shrugged at all this. They accepted the lies and refused to believe what their own eyes were telling them.

Even more egregious than the male Moroccan milers, the female Chinese 10,000-meter runners, and the left fielders from California, however, were the professional cyclists in the Tour de France peloton, who blasted up 11,000-foot Alpine peaks without popping a sweat and who enlisted platoons of doctors, trainers, and handlers to administer erythropoietin (the notorious EPO, which boosted red blood cell counts and illicitly improved athletic endurance) injections and complex regimes of blood doping. Finally, in 1998, the French-based Festina team was so blatant in its doping, so brazen in its system, that they got popped, arrested by French customs agents as their car was returning to France from Belgium, where a stage of the Tour de France had just taken place. The Festina affair pulled back the curtain, exposing the tawdry truth about professional sports.

In Boulder, I watched these developments with interest but at a certain remove. Just as my gold medal run in Munich had helped spark the 1970s running boom, my silver medal run in Montreal behind East German team member Cierpinski had dramatically opened the performance-enhancing drug era of sports in general and Olympic-level distance running in particular. But again, I was determined not to come across as a whining sore loser, pathetically crying cheater. There was no proof to back my conviction that Cierpinski had juiced, and I possessed no agency or authority to do anything about it even if there was solid evidence, especially after all these years.

Periodically a reporter would call, asking if, given all the doping news, I had launched a campaign to have the 1976 Marathon medal results overturned. I always replied no, there was no point in that, which was true. It was also true that just as I had repressed virtually all thoughts of the man who had stolen my innocence and my childhood, I gave not a thought to Waldemar Cierpinski, the man who many people around the world believed had stolen my gold medal.

The Festina affair unfolded with a great deal of smoke and little fire. After a slew of investigations and many passionate pledges of reform, the public and media lost interest. The few riders who'd been busted were reinstated, soon to be joined by an even more cynical and diabolical cheater. In the late 1990s, a cancer survivor from Texas named Lance Armstrong started soaring up those 11,000-foot peaks as if they were surface-street speed bumps, glancing back at his pursuers the way Cierpinski had looked back at me during the marathon in Montreal.

And then, similar to the case of my marathon in Munich, history intervened. Domestic and international political forces gave the wheel a shove. Late in 1998, after the Festina affair that summer, I read that the Office of National Drug Control Policy, an arm of the federal executive branch, had committed 1 million dollars to develop a test for EPO. I wrote a letter to Gen. Barry McCafferey, the Office of National Drug Control Policy head, thanking him and offering my expertise and advice. I wrote a similar letter to President Clinton.

I realized that if there was any chance of making a dent in the performance-enhancing drug edifice, the attack would have to originate from an independent group with enforcement powers. Asking individual sports to continue to police their own athletes' drug abuse was tantamount to inviting the fox to guard the chicken coop.

Meanwhile, events occuring halfway around the world would also deepen my involvement in the anti-doping cause. Werner Franke was a distinguished biochemist in both the Soviet Bloc East Germany and the newly reunified nation. Dr. Franke served as the lead researcher at Germany's National Cancer Institute and was a professor at Heidelberg University. His wife, Brigitte Berendonk, was a former Olympian in the shot put and discus.

Competing for East Germany in the 1960s and '70s, Berendonk refused to juice—she did not accept the steroid injections ordered by the commissars in her nation's sports academies—and thus suffered doubly. She could not match the performances of her steroid-queen countrywomen and therefore failed to attain full extension in the sport she loved. And now in middle age, after the nation's reunification, when the anabolic-laced East German athlete had turned into a global stereotype and running joke, everyone assumed that Berendonk had been one of those steroid queens. Perhaps she would soon develop cancer or some other juice-related disease.

After the collapse of the Berlin Wall, around 1990, Berendonk started looking for documentation proving the extent and severity of the East German doping system, only to be stymied by a figurative wall. Officials told her that all of the incriminating documents had been destroyed, much in the way that the pencil-thin mustached, doping maestro Victor Conte dumped incriminating records in the trash behind his Balco lab in California 20 years later.

But then her husband, Dr. Franke, got on the case. Stepping away from the laboratory but deeper into his role as a seeker of objective, disinterested truth, Dr. Franke methodically started to investigate the history of the vast East German sports-doping edifice. It was a task at once daunting and straightforward, not unlike the fall of the physical Berlin Wall itself. Seemingly inviolate, as permanent as the Great Wall of China and defended with the full weight of a mighty empire, the wall had disintegrated with shocking velocity, starting with one brick being dislodged and then accelerating into a giant pile, opening a gaping hole through which the citizens of a newly liberated republic soon moved freely back and forth. For a long time, the wall surrounding the state-sponsored East German doping system proved more complicated to breach.

Dr. Franke persevered, however, and through a series of cloak-and-dagger machinations, he discovered that a mass of data from that era had been photocopied. Through friends of friends, Dr. Franke and Berendonk got their hands on the documents, which definitively proved that the system was far more extensive, and far more central to the East German government, than was even imagined during the cold war era.

The nation's leaders judged Olympic sports to be of paramount importance. During the 1970s, a full 2 percent of East Germany's annual budget was dedicated to its sports program. Coaches, doctors, and managers weren't merely encouraged to administer performance-enhancing drugs; they were required to do so by secret law. The Stasi, the notorious national spy agency, controlled much of the action, and many of the juiced athletes served as paid Stasi agents and informers.

Although accused of being traitors and threatened with reprisals, Dr. Franke and Berendonk went public with their findings, publishing a bestselling book. And through the 1990s they continued with their research, now aided by a number of disaffected former athletes, many of whom were suffering serious health problems due to years of performance-enhancing drug abuse. When McCaffrey stated an interest in battling sports doping as part of the DEA mandate, my interest in the German couple's work intensified. In January of 1998, I saw that Dr. Franke would be visiting Colorado to speak at a meeting of the US Olympic Committee in Colorado Springs. I contacted the scientist and arranged to have dinner with him during his stay.

The scene of our meeting was befitting the spy-movie vibe of much of Dr. Franke's investigation—the Broadmoor Hotel in Colorado Springs, a grand, old resort hotel built in the 1920s that would look at home in the Dolomites as well as the Rockies. And Herr Doktor Franke looked like a professor from central casting, dignified but approachable, with elegant old-world manners leavened by a dry sense of humor. I started to introduce myself to the professor, but he stopped me. "I know who you are," he said. I started to explain about the '76 Olympic Marathon, and again he held his hand up. "I know all about Mr. Cierpinski," he said.

The question was, what did *I* want to know about Waldemar Cierpinski? I didn't seek retribution, I didn't want him to be punished, and I didn't want to have the marathon medals be redistributed: I just wanted to know if there was evidence supporting what everybody already knew; I wanted this man's secret to be exposed; I wanted proof that I'd gotten this one right.

Dr. Franke heard me out and said he thought he might have something for me. He said he would be in touch soon after his return to Europe. We finished dinner and shook hands, and I watched the professor disappear into the Broadmoor elevator.

I drove back to Boulder, returned to my routine, and went back to my office at Frank Shorter Sports headquarters. Dr. Franke was an extremely busy man. Perhaps he would forget to get in touch at all; his offer to help was the kind of thing you say in the pulse of the moment when you're traveling and tend to put off and eventually forget about when you get back home. By now I was growing accustomed to all manner of evasions of the truth, from the cynical, pervasive organized criminal lying of nation states to the denial of individuals caught up in those systems to the psychopathic lying of people such as my father to the instinctive denial with which we all respond to inconvenient truths and uncomfortable facts.

On the other hand, Dr. Franke was a serious man of integrity with a personal stake in this game. He understood denial and falsehood at least as well as I did; indeed, that mutual understanding seemed to form an unspoken bond as we dined together that winter night at the Broadmoor. And sure enough, less than a week after meeting the professor, I was in my office when a multipage fax came in from Heidelberg.

I ripped the pages from the fax machine; at first, they were difficult to decipher. The words, some typed, others handwritten, were all in German, bearing the official stamp of the Stasi. From the professor's brief cover letter and on closer examination, I was able to determine that the documents were minutes of a high-level meeting regarding the doping regimen of elite Olympic athletes. In characteristic Teutonic fashion, the report went into specific detail about the types of drugs to be administered and even listed the dosages.

I leafed through the pages and near the end of the pile, hit the mother lode: a clearly legible handwritten list of the athletes enrolled in the program. I recognized many of the names—members of the infamous East German swim team, the women with linebacker shoulders who set world records every time they jumped in the pool and who appeared as blatant in their cheating as the Festina cyclists would appear a generation later. I worked down the rows of names. Midway down the row, I stopped. There, number 62: Waldemar Cierpinski followed by the notation, the same in German as in English: marathon.

A thrill shot through me. After 20 years of biting my tongue, I finally had something meaningful to talk about. I felt a range of emotions, but the strongest was relief. The suspicion—the knowledge—that I'd been carrying around for 22 years had been corroborated. Seeing his name on that list satisfied the lawyer in me. Cierpinski was not the only track-and-field athlete on the list, but apparently, he had been handpicked for the program—specifically chosen to defeat the American defending champion in the event.

Besides exposing Cierpinski as number 62 in the list of 143 athletes mentioned by name in State Plan 14.25, Dr. Franke, along with Western journalists who followed up on his research, uncovered further information about the East German marathoner. Beginning in 1973, when he was still an anonymous, undistinguished steeplechaser, Cierpinski became a documented spy and informer for the Stasi, the East German secret police. Apparently, his tasks included reporting on fellow athletes who were contemplating, thinking, or simply dreaming of defecting to the West.

Many other East German athletes accepted similar Stasi assignments, but others refused to spy on their fellow athletes. After winning the gold medal in Montreal, moreover, Cierpinski became a Communist Party member. He quoted Karl Marx and gave speeches at Communist Party congresses. His Olympic gold medal performances made him a national hero in East Germany. He was twice voted that nation's athlete of the year. After his triumph at the '80 Games in Moscow, an enraptured East German TV announcer exhorted his audience: "Fathers, have courage! Name your sons Waldemar!"

Unlike some of his fellow athletes, Cierpinski couldn't claim that he'd been an unwilling dupe of the system or that his coach had told him that the steroid pills were merely vitamins. Cierpinski couldn't get off by claiming he was just following orders.

Part of me wanted to respond in the manner of Don Kardong, whom many assumed to be the rightful bronze medalist at the Montreal Marathon. Once Cierpinski showed up as number 62 on the list, Don argued vehemently and cogently in the media and to the International Association of Athletics (IAAF) to have the East German's Olympic performance struck from the books, similar to the way that the medals illicitly won in '76 had been stripped from East German swimmers. "I've been cheated for 22 years," Don pointed out to a *Wall Street Journal* reporter in 1998.

Ultimately, however, I chose to follow a different path. With my contacts and legal training, I understood the way the US Olympic Committee (USOC) and IAAF functioned—or more often failed to function. Despite the evidence, the governing bodies said flat out they were not interested in rewriting Olympic history. They cited legal and jurisdictional issues, many of them legitimate. How could you prove that Cierpinski wasn't coerced to dope? For that matter, how could you produce the mass of hard evidence that would unequivocally prove that he had juiced? That required more than a handwritten name on a list.

No, there wasn't much of a percentage, and less of a shot at satisfaction, in going after Cierpinski personally. "What's important for me is the deterrence aspect," I told the *Wall Street Journal* reporter. "It may take a while, but you will get caught."

In short, I wasn't going to use Dr. Franke's information to mount a campaign to have Cierpinski's gold medal rescinded. Instead, I would employ the evidence in an effort to reframe the event and move forward. Maybe we could build something sturdy that could be of use to others. I was thinking about honorable athletes such as Jack Bacheler and Steve Prefontaine, whose sacrifices and values had been trashed. I was thinking about elite and professional-level athletes who had been cheated out of medals and thousands of dollars of income—athletes such as Don Kardong. But I was also thinking about the kids you never hear about, the ones discouraged from trying out for the team because they knew they couldn't compete with the cheaters—the runners whose names didn't show up in the newspaper to make their parents proud.

I thought about McCaffrey, the drug czar. I thought about the French customs agents stopping the Festina support vehicle and discovering a trunk full of hypodermic needles and EPO on ice. And then I remembered my run three years earlier with President Clinton. A man named Bob Weiner, a devoted distance runner, had served on the White Houase staff and now worked for General McCaffrey. Wheels started to turn. I followed the web that running weaves.

I sat down and drafted a three-page memo, outlining the fundamentals for an anti-doping policy that could be enacted by an independent, stand-alone agency within the auspices of the DEA. The program would be based on deterrence rather than punishment. Testing and enforcement would be conducted by an independent, government-funded agency rather than by officials within the individual sport. The testing would occur without notice and outside of competition on an unannounced, random basis. Test results would indicate an athlete's physiological baseline over time, and a sudden change to that baseline would raise red flags.

I sent the letter off and didn't think much about it, assuming it would lie forgotten under a mountain of paper on an overworked bureaucrat's desk. But a few days later, in a bolt from the blue like the Dr. Franke fax, I got a call from Bob Weiner.

"Frank, the general really liked your proposal," Weiner said. "We ran it by the president and he liked it, too. He would like you to write up a more detailed outline and then come to Washington and talk it over."

That and subsequent meetings eventually led to the creation of the US Anti-Doping Agency (USADA). I was directly involved in the planning process. I had input on the organizational structure and the decision to support Dick Pound as the head of the World Anti-Doping Agency, which would be based in Montreal. After the plan was accepted by the International Olympic Committee I thought my work was done, but General McCafferey asked the USOC to allow me to serve on the original USADA board. At the incorporation meeting, I went out for a run at lunchtime and returned to discover that I'd been elected chairman of the board of directors in my absence.

+ + +

I knew what I was getting myself into. I knew I wouldn't be in control. I had been around enough people in government, corporations, and other organizations. I understood the arc of these new enterprises. You rode in on a wave of energy and enthusiasm and hope—the belief that this time the outcome would be different. Honest people had come into power, and justice would be served. I knew this first burst of energy would inevitably fade, but it was still necessary at the start. Otherwise, why start in the first place? "Readiness is all," I had read in the Shakespeare assigned to me back in the Great Books course I took during my freshman year at Yale, and ever since then, I had put that precept to practical use.

In my marathons I timed my surges and retreats down to the second, understanding their psychological as well as physical implications. As an undergraduate I had avoided the marches and protests, choosing to bide my time and accrue power and step forward when I could exert maximum leverage and influence. In the matter of fighting doping, the optimal time to start would have been 20 years earlier, but now would have to do. Doping was everywhere, and fans and the media were finally starting to see what was in front of their noses.

So I approached the job as if it were a race. Ride that early energy. Yahoo the start so you don't get buried in the slop and roil of that first mile. The USADA, the first agency of its kind and the template for the World Anti-Doping Agency, came into being in February 2000, with yours truly serving as the chairman of the board of directors. I had credibility because I was generally perceived as an honest Olympic gold medalist in the marathon; because the 1976 and 1980 gold medalist had been documented to be Number 62 in the list of athletes enumerated in East German State Plan 14:25.

From the start we were a truly independent agency, in charge of testing and adjudicating penalties and appeals up to the Supreme

Court of Sport. USADA was also responsible for research and education. The emphasis was on deterring future cheaters at a young age by showing that USADA was serious about detecting and penalizing cheaters among elite athletes.

Still, there was a gap between the public's perception of USADA and the operational reality. Our funding was meager, just a few million dollars annually, indicating the tendency of the big players to appear as if they were concerned about the juicing problem without committing adequate resources. Our agency occupied murky jurisdictional territory; we weren't fully vested as an arm of the Department of Justice. The energy and talent focused on testing and detection were a laughable fraction of what the cheaters were devoting to their craft. Yet despite these limitations and compromises, I embraced the task, working both openly and behind the scenes, speaking to the public and media about the issue.

I tried to keep our original goals in focus, the main points I had emphasized in my memo to General Barry McCaffrey after I had met with Dr. Franke and seen the Stasi document. Testing and enforcement had to remain independent of the individual sports federations, and we needed to place an emphasis on deterring future juicers rather than punishing the proven ones. All parties agreed on the second goal: No one wanted to see their heroes tarnished unless it was absolutely necessary, unless their cheating was unequivocal and could be decisively proven—a high bar indeed. But the first goal—a truly independent agency, amply funded, with real enforcement clout—proved more difficult to implement. The reason wasn't hard to fathom: Nobody wanted to yield their own little (or not so little) fiefdoms of power and money.

The doping problem was much worse than anyone could imagine. In both track and road racing, there was almost no chance for a clean runner to succeed in any major competition. The level of denial and duplicity was galling. Many of the athletes who presented the shiniest image—who railed publicly against doping, insisting that they ran clean—were, in fact, the most corrupt and inveterate juicers. In my capacity as chairman of the USADA board, I had to appear with them on stage. I had to present them with awards and sing their praises to the media.

Eventually, it got to be too much for me. I grew more barbed and pointed in my public comments. I declined to appear at functions honoring coaches, agents, and athletes who I knew were cheating. Working a telecast of a road race or track meet, I would point out the dopers to my colleagues during commercial breaks; on air, I found it more and more difficult to refrain from doing the same for our viewers. I began to chafe at the delays and evasions. I despaired at the endemic corruption of the sport that I loved but had trouble convincing others that elite-level running was in crisis.

I argued that if a performance seemed too good to be true—a sub-30-minute 10-K by a woman, for instance, or a 2:02 marathon by a man—it almost certainly was too good to be true. I insisted that despite all the advances in technology and sports science, distance running remained the most basic of sports, and that when coaches, agents, and athletes talked of its complexity, they were usually using complexity as a smokescreen.

People started to edge away from me at cocktail parties. They whispered that I'd turned paranoid. Dick Ebersol at NBC, my old Yale buddy, stopped returning my calls. My TV commentating gigs dried up.

In 2003, I decided to leave the board. The day-to-day operations were being expertly handled by Terry Madden, our CEO, and Travis Tygart, who had just come on board as an in-house attorney. The structure and policy had been solidly established and our reputation was growing. My role was mainly in the start-up phase: attracting public and political attention and lending credibility to the effort. After resigning from the board, I continued to serve as a de facto spokesman for USADA, giving media interviews and working to keep doping issues out in the open, in the public eye.

And how about Waldemar Cierpinski? I hadn't followed the man's post-running career closely, but I heard that he'd been successful. His sporting goods stores were thriving in the robust German economy. He was still cashing in on his celebrity and on those Olympic gold medals that no one had been able to take away from him. He continued to deny that he'd doped. Every so often a journalist would challenge him on his performance at the Montreal Games and on his name appearing in State Plan 14.25, but Cierpinski generally declined interview requests.

"These accusations are absurd," he complained to a reporter in 1999. "I'm confronted every other day with something like this. It's aggravating."

Good, I thought, standing at the kitchen window with my cup of cold coffee. The guy deserves to be aggravated. I understood that Cierpinski's son was a national-class marathoner and triathlete. I wondered what the young man thought about his father. I wondered what the father told his son or what sorts of stories he would tell his grandchildren. I wondered how Cierpinski was able to live with his ghosts.

For decades, I had been haunted by the memory of Cierpinski looking back at me at the 21-mile mark in Montreal, then turning and rocketing away. By speaking out on behalf of honest athletes who didn't have a platform and by establishing the framework for USADA, I had done my best to lay that ghost to rest. I suspected that, for his part, Waldemar Cierpinski had never stopped looking back over his shoulder.

21

That's My Story

I had outrun one ghost, but another was still hanging around. I thought I'd put my father to rest on that June evening in 2008, when I left the house on Wisner Avenue in Middletown. I had broken out of the musty sickroom, redolent of disinfectant and death and emerged into an evening, fragrant with lilac and honeysuckle. My father was gone, and he couldn't hurt anyone again.

I had gone back to my life. The silence and distance continued with my siblings, but I couldn't expect that to change overnight. I returned to default mode, not thinking about my father, not thinking about those long-ago nights when the man climbed the stairs, not thinking about all the times when I pulled at his arm, begging him to stop wailing on Mary or Nanette or Chris or Barbara—my father would just swat me away and carry on with the pounding.

During the months after my father's death, however, my default not-thinking mode began to wobble. Shards of memory bobbed to the surface at unexpected moments: while I ran the trails around Wonderland Lake; as I stood in line to board a flight to a race or a speaking gig; as I drove across town to the post office or cycled down to the market for something to cook for dinner. There was no stopping or derailing the memories. They seemed to rise and take shape with a force and trajectory of their own. At first, I tried to resist the images, force them back down into my unconscious, but over time I learned to accept them. The flow of memories was trying to tell me something, take me somewhere, and goad me toward some action. But as of yet that message, and my mission, remained unclear.

Early in November 2010, about a month before Mac called from Fort Wayne, I traveled to a road race speaking engagement in Springfield, Missouri. Springfield is a heartland city of 100,000, struggling like most American cities of its type, with factories and railroad yards closing and hospitals and the government now providing the bulk of the employment. The city had one good economic thing going for it, however—the Bass Pro Shops, the largest outdoor sports retailer in America. The company was putting on a fitness weekend centered on a 10-K road race. To appear at the accompanying expo, Bass had brought in Bill Rodgers, Dick Beardsley, and myself.

Our hosts took the three of us out to visit Boys and Girls Town, one of the charities that the race was benefiting, which turned out to be a residential center for delinquent youths. Fate was intervening, as history had intervened in Munich and Montreal. We were three aging warriors, each of us dinged and scarred. Besides our decades-long athletic rivalry, Rodgers and I had once feuded in business. Like me, Bill operated a running apparel line, and along with his brother Charlie owned a popular running specialty store in his native Boston.

Dick Beardsley was slightly younger than Rodgers and me, but he had suffered more. After his thrilling race with Salazar at the 1982 Boston Marathon, Dick had been hammered by one terrible misfortune after another, from a near-fatal farm accident to felony opiate addiction. And, like Rodgers and me, Beardsley had dealt honorably with the pain and fatigue of the marathon. Indeed, although we had each arrived at a relatively comfortable middle age, the three of us were brothers in pain.

At the residential center we were supposed to meet some of the kids, and each of us would deliver a brief motivational talk. I had given that speech many times with slight variations during my career, and so had Dick and Bill. As we sat on the stage as our host introduced us, I felt the same loosening, the same slippage of my heart, that I'd felt when I had visited my father on the day before he died. I looked out at our audience, at all of those beat-up kids, and I realized that we belonged to the same veteran's organization.

Bill went first. His talk was a little rambling, as was his style, but his sincerity came through, and the kids listened intently. There was no accounting for charisma, for natural warmth and the ability to connect. The kids engaged even more deeply with Dick, whose rending tale of addiction and recovery struck a chord in that small city just beginning to be raked by opiate abuse.

I was sort of half-listening to Beardsley. With the other half of my mind, I should have been planning what I was going to say. I always planned, always plotted, always rehearsed. But on this afternoon, for some reason, that part of my mind had gone blank. No sentences, no words, no themes. I just kept looking out at the kids. Each of them, I suspected, had been betrayed and abused in some fundamental manner by the people close to them. Their confinement in this facility indicated that they were heading down a path in which they might betray and abuse others in turn.

Finally, it was my turn to speak. My mind was still blank. Dick and Bill had already talked about perseverance and goal setting, and the kids expected more of the same from me. I started that talk, that set piece, but then halted. There was an awkward beat of silence. I felt Beardsley and Rodgers watching me, waiting for me to continue in my usual role as the father of the running boom.

I cleared my throat. And then, instead of my standard motivational rap, I started talking about my boyhood, about growing up in a town not so different from Springfield. I talked about growing up with a father who was an actor, a handsome, charming, diabolical actor. I talked about lying in bed and hearing my father's footsteps on the stairs. I recalled going out on house calls with my doctor father when I was 9 years old. I remembered a day when a neighbor lady saw my father and me getting into the station wagon. The lady had smiled down at me and said, "When you grow up, I bet you're going to become a doctor, just like your daddy!"

I talked about trying to anticipate my father's moods and movements, the enormous effort it took to keep out of his way and to help my sisters and brothers do the same. I remembered my mother's fear and silence. I talked about my desire to escape. I talked about searching for an outlet for my fear and anger and finding it in running. I talked about the guilt I felt for surviving, for not doing a better job of saving the rest of my family.

Usually I spoke deliberately, but today it came in a rush—no pacing, no orderly marshalling of facts. It seemed as if I was in two places at once, at the lectern speaking and standing apart from myself. Normally, along with carefully planning my talks and tailoring my message to the particular audience, I made a point of reading the room; that is, sensing the response of my listeners and making the subsequent adjustments. But today, at the detention center, I made no attempt to read the room.

There were moments when I wasn't even aware of the audience, when I felt alone, making my confession to the entity I had encountered as a young man when I ran the Taos ski mountain in the glow of luminous, red-gold sunsets. At other moments during the talk, as I paused to absorb another blast of memory, I was intensely, almost painfully aware of the kids.

"I've known Frank for years, and I had never heard any of this," Dick Beardsley told a reporter later. "None of us had. We were shocked. Bill Rodgers always looks sort of dazed, but he looked more dazed than usual. Suddenly some things made sense about Frank. I had always felt this sense of aloofness and distance from him—sometimes he would look at me like he didn't even know me. I thought it was something I had done. I talked to friends about it, and they said don't take it personally, that's just Frank. But sitting there on that stage, listening to Frank talk about his father coming up the stairs and deciding which of his kids he was going to wail on, I suddenly understood where his distance came from."

At the end of my talk, I felt spent, empty, and exhausted, the way I used to feel after a draining interval session on the track. Rodgers and Beardsley went out to the parking lot with our host, letting me engage the line of kids waiting to greet me. There were at least a dozen, and they approached respectfully. None of the kids lingered long, and none tried to start a conversation. Just a touch, a glancing meeting of eyes, a quick, mumbled thank you.

I finished with the line and was gathering my belongings when a girl approached. I had seen her at the end of the line a moment ago, but I assumed she had changed her mind and had decided to leave. Now I realized that she was waiting to meet me privately. She appeared to be around 14. She said her name, but I failed to register it. Our eyes met, and then the girl looked away. I again thought she was going to leave, but instead she gathered herself.

"That story you told," she said. "That's my story. All of those things happened to me. The way you tried to keep one step ahead of your father and worried about your sisters and brothers—that was me you were talking about."

That day, that girl, snapped my feelings into focus. I had a responsibility to tell my story, which could be of use to people like this young woman. For my whole adult life I'd been explaining things to people, from the healing power of the marathon to the corrosive danger of performance-enhancing drugs. All of that explaining, and I had never explained the central fact of my own life—to others, or to myself.

Word of my unexpected confession got out, as I suspected it would, and before long a writer from *Runner's World* gave me a call, wanting to profile me in light of my revelations. I told him I would think it over.

Did I want to bring the story of my father all the way out into the open? Did I want to risk being lumped in with the afternoon talk-show crowd? Did I want to peel away the emotional scar tissue that had cushioned me all these years? And say I did agree to the project—when the reporter came to interview me, what if I froze up? What if the memories stayed repressed and sealed? What if I again failed to shape my father's crimes into a coherent narrative?

On the other hand, now that I had started the process, given the wheel a shove, I felt compelled to see it through to a resolution. I always hated dropping out of a race, and I had never started a hard workout without completing it. Moreover, I was curious. As always, I wanted to find out. I wanted to believe in my own story. The crimes of my father had been so long repressed, had been crammed for so long inside my heart and mind and those of my sisters and brothers; they were so at odds with the persona that my father presented to the world that I sometimes doubted my own judgment. Perhaps if I related them to a reporter, and eventually saw them depicted in print, I would see the crimes in a true light.

I brooded over these questions through the holiday season of 2010, around the time that Mac called, inviting me to Fort Wayne. I was still reluctant to commit, even though my session back in Springfield in November had essentially settled the matter. I knew why I wanted to talk. I would just have to trust that when I stepped to the line, I'd have something to say. Early in January I e-mailed the writer, agreeing to an interview, and on a cold, bright morning during the first weeks of 2011, he and I started talking in the kitchen of my house in Boulder, on the shore of Wonderland Lake, by the network of trails carrying into the foothills. As we talked, the runners and walkers pulsed by, and as the morning deepened, the sky darkened, storm clouds boiled over the Flatirons, and thick drapes of snow began to fall.

At first, the memories came out with staccato timing and in a spectral light, conforming to no orderly chronology, often repeating, broken by long pauses and silences, but by the afternoon they had started to flow. I found a kind of rhythm. The house on Highland Avenue gradually took shape. Dr. Sam stepped out of the shadows and up the stairs from the kitchen, belt in hand, calling the name of his night's victim.

After two draining days of interviews, the writer went home, and I returned to my routine—morning hours of e-mail correspondence and phone business, a workout, lunch, more business, an afternoon workout—the same basic schedule I'd been following since my senior year at Yale. I traveled to the Rock 'n' Roll Marathon in New Orleans to give a talk at the expo.

When I returned to Boulder, I received a call from the writer. The story was looking good, he said, but the magazine couldn't publish it without corroboration. My father, obviously, wasn't alive to respond to my testimony. The writer wanted—needed—to talk to my sisters.

I immediately and adamantly refused. This was my story, my attempt at justice. I was not about to ask my sisters to open their old wounds for the sake of my agenda. I would not grant permission for the writer to talk to my sisters.

There was silence on the line. "Would you think about it?" he asked finally.

I said I would, and a few days later I departed for my engagement in Fort Wayne.

✦ ✦ ✦

At the end of January 2011, I flew out of Denver International, bound for the cold heartland—Indiana in midwinter. You might think I'd find such small-market jobs tiresome, tasks to endure, but I enjoyed them. I liked to follow the web that the sport weaved, learning about a running community, meeting the players, recognizing the similarities and patterns between now and the scene 40 years ago. A running community still relied on its leaders, a few key people with imagination and vision—the model of Jimmy Carnes, of Fred Lebow, of Steve Bosley repeating in the 21st century.

So I looked forward to the weekend and welcomed the payday. I was helping my daughter with her vet school tuition and my son with his law school tuition and expenses. I supported my kids unreservedly. I had attended as many events as I could and wholeheartedly backed every one of their interests. And, of course, I had never, ever raised a hand to them.

Another reason to welcome this trip: the time and space to think. Should I let the writer talk to my sisters about Dr. Sam?

How could I best serve and protect my siblings? How much of the past did I want to open? Did I really want to relive my lifelong family train wreck? On the other hand, was it really up to me to decide if my sisters wanted to talk?

Mac picked me up at the small regional airport in Fort Wayne and drove me into town. He apologized for the bleak, gray afternoon, for the cliffs of dirty snow lining the roadside, and for the downtown's empty sidewalks and vacant storefronts. He explained that Fort Wayne was a Rust Belt city that had once thrived, thanks to the American automotive industry. Maybe I was old enough to remember the Fort Wayne Pistons, one of the charter teams of the NBA?

"It might not look like it, but we've come a long way in the last few years," Mac said.

"Hey, no need to apologize," I said. "I already like this place." That was true. In fact, Fort Wayne reminded me of a bigger Middletown.

Mac pulled up to a pleasant ranch-style house in a suburban cul de sac, where the snow was deeper and cleaner than in town and was piled up near the tops of the mailboxes. And now, as dusk clamped down, snowflakes flitted and slanted in the beam of the SUV headlights. My hosts, a top masters runner in the area who operated a successful insurance business and his wife, greeted me at the door. The couple explained that their son—a star high school runner soon off to college—would come by later with a few of his teammates. The boys were eager to meet me, the man said.

Before dinner, I stretched out on the bed in the guest room. Pellets of snow ticked against the window. I closed my eyes. I couldn't sleep, but it felt good to shut down briefly and plan what I wanted to say that night and the next day both at brunch and during the speech and formal dinner. With the exception of that day in Springfield the previous November, I always planned my talks, no matter how large or small the audience. It was a carryover from my competitive running career, when every workout had had a specific purpose, as did every mile or repeat during the workout. I had a few set pieces and themes I could adapt to almost any occasion. Most recently, given my work with the US Anti-Doping Agency (USADA), I would deliver a doping-related talk. I suspected, however, that only a few people in the Fort Wayne crowd would be interested in that topic.

My hosts in the track club were part of the citizen-runner scene, which was burgeoning, even in an economically struggling town such as Fort Wayne. A worker laid off from her job might not be able to afford a gym membership, but she could always invest in a pair of running shoes. The split was still there between the bright realm of the citizen-runners and the shadowed world of the elites, and the chasm seemed to be growing wider and deeper.

So no doping tonight. I would explore other themes—Munich and Pre and motivational stories for the high school kids. Lying on the bed, listening to the wind rattle the window, I tried to follow these threads, to fasten on phrases and words to get me started. But my mind kept sliding back to thoughts of my father. I worried about what I'd told the writer. Had I come across as just another self-absorbed Baby Boomer?

The Boomers: the generation that brought you televised urban terrorism and the marathon. What if all my remembering and confessing was just for my own benefit, a way to still matter? What was I doing to my sisters? Did they deserve to scratch for my itch? Or was I being too hard on myself?

The questions kept turning in my mind, and the snow kept ticking at the window; finally, I fell into a brief, shallow sleep.

A half hour later my hosts called me for dinner. I was the guest of honor, first through the line, first to scoop the macaroni casserole in the brightly lit kitchen. My host had invited four other guests, pals from his days as a local high school runner, along with their retired coach. We sat around the kitchen table—the guys got an hour with me before the high school kids arrived. It felt like one of those scenes during presidential campaigns, when the candidate billets for the night at a home of an "average voter." The news photos show the candidate sitting at the kitchen table without a tie, his sleeves rolled up, sharing a meat loaf supper with his hosts while talking over bread and butter economic issues.

But the difference was, I wasn't running for office. I didn't want anything from these people around the table. I was truly interested in interacting with these runners from my era who shared my "disease." We all loved to run and to talk about our training, racing, and injuries. This gathering was a lot like my annual Hood to Coast Relay weekend with my old Yale buddies—same feeling, just different group.

We made small talk about the weather and about famous Indianans. I learned that James Dean came from a little town just down the highway. After a few minutes the attention focused on me. Mindful of my running-savvy audience, I mentioned that my first national-class race had happened at this time of year, the 10,000 meters at the NCAA Indoor Championships at Detroit's Joe Louis Arena in 1969.

That ignited a gleam in the old coach's eye. He had been there, he said; the coach had been at that meet. For the next 15 minutes, I riffed on my favorite subject: training philosophy. Before the gold medal, before getting anointed the father of the boom, before the TV commentary, the apparel company, and the USADA chairmanship, I had been a hopelessly devoted track geek.

These men were fellow connoisseurs, so I could get specific, discussing my ideas in detail: Amass a high-volume, high-quality weekly mileage; log two hard track workouts during the week; and on the weekend knock out a long run at an aerobic pace adjusted to the perceived effort of the shorter work. I talked about peaking and discussed how I had timed my midrace surges. I talked about that mythical, magical, invisible 10-meter thread that connected the hare and the hound; once the hare broke that thread, he was gone. The detailed craft talk might have seemed disconnected to my other themes, but in my mind it was all connected: Assiduously practicing the craft of running sat at the heart of everything I'd accomplished during my career.

"My absolute favorite workout?" I said, responding to a question. "The one that showed the true state of my fitness? That would be 6 × 800 meters at a pace faster than 5000-meter race pace, with as little recovery as possible between each rep." The guys sagely nodded. I could have continued happily in this vein for hours, but as our hostess cleared the table, an expectant silence built. I knew it was time to shift gears.

"Frank, I never quite understood," one of the guests said. "At Munich in '72, did you know what was happening during the terrorist attacks?"

The wheels turned in my brain: the Munich massacre, the morning after the break-in. I began by setting the scene at our apartment in the athletes' village. I explained that I had been sleeping out on the balcony, on a mattress on the floor, because Dave Wottle and his bride had taken over my bedroom. Dave had already won his gold medal in the 800 meters and was in party mode, I told the guys.

The guys' faces went slack with pleasure as they pictured the scene, one that had unfolded four decades ago but that still some-

times felt like a century, given how far we'd advanced in the intervening years. Or, by another reckoning, how far we had fallen.
Today, during an Olympic competition, US runners prepare for
their events at first-class resorts and fly in on chartered jets the day
before the race. They sleep in air-conditioned hyperbaric comfort
and eat organic locally sourced meals, calibrated to the last gram
of fat and protein.

In 1972 I slept on a mattress on the concrete floor of an open-
air porch, looking into the courtyard of the apartment complex in
the Olympic Village. Although I had hardly felt deprived. I was
pleased and proud to be there with Pre and Kenny Moore, my
friends and training partners, who were also my mentors and role
models. A mattress on the porch was all I needed. And as it turned
out, I explained to my dinner companions in Fort Wayne, that
humble perch had given me a good view—perhaps too good a
view—of the unfolding catastrophe.

"We could see and hear the helicopters," I told the guys. "We
looked across the courtyard, and there was one of the terrorists in
a balaclava, standing on the balcony with his rifle."

A rapt silence filled the kitchen. I continued the story, telling
how we had spent that day huddled around the TV, with Steve
Prefontaine translating the German news bulletins. I described the
turmoil as the action moved to the airport; the brief hope flaring
when it seemed that the situation might resolve without violence;
and finally, the despair when the news arrived that the authorities
had attacked out at the airport, and 11 athletes had perished.

I explained how we had had to interpret and process those
developments while at the same time trying to prepare for our
events. I related my conversation with Kenny Moore: Kenny telling
me that he'd run in tribute to and in memory of the fallen athletes.

I explained that I chose to honor the dead by not giving them a thought, by channeling all my energy and anxiety and turmoil into running my marathon.

My small audience, guys around my own age, hung on my words. Yet at the same time, you could almost hear their brains churning. They were listening to me, the man who had been in Munich, but they were also remembering where they had been on the day that I was describing. They were likely recalling details from their pasts in the way that I recalled the flickering picture of our black-and-white TV in our apartment in the athlete's village. Maybe they were remembering the aroma of candles in a college dorm room, or a VW bug with a troublesome clutch, or a green-eyed girl in patched Levis who waited tables at the student union: the seemingly unrelated people and things they forever associated with that watershed day in 1972.

The men around the table in Fort Wayne remembered following the developments of the Munich Massacre on TV or over their car radios: a moment that changed the texture of modern life, weaving a thread of uncertainty and fear. They also remembered the moment five days after the Munich Massacre, when they gathered around a TV set to watch the Olympic Marathon, the race that had inspired their own running, opening a trail that had carried through the years, eventually delivering them to this moment.

I wrapped up the story of Munich, 1972. The men departed, and the high school kids piled in from out of the cold.

During the intermission I rose from the table, stretched my stiff back, and rubbed my sore hip. I scooped up a handful of peanut M&M's from a bowl on the coffee table. I was enjoying myself. I liked doing these gigs—hitting a rhythm, sensing when to surge, when to back off. In some ways the performance resembled a marathon. I munched on the candy and said hello to the high school kids and their parents. As we took our seats in the living room, somebody said that today would have been Steve Prefontaine's birthday.

I settled in with the kids—three seniors in high school, among the best prep distance runners in the state of Indiana. They had stars in their eyes and the world at their feet. They sat down to listen to the old man, a relic of the 20th century.

Teenagers are notorious for zoning out at such moments, but the boys heard me out attentively. Like most runners under age 40, they knew me mainly through the character portrayed in *Without Limits*, the movie about Pre. I was Frank Shorter, the guy with the toothache whom Pre had driven home from the party before augering into the rock.

"My progression was just like yours," I told the boys. "I never had the idea that I was going to be the best. My goal was to try to get to the next level. I didn't need to win; I needed to find out if I had gotten my training right. It never bothered me to lose. I reframed my losses. The only way you can get better is to lose."

I emphasized three points: Make running fun, the thing you turn to for release; approach running as an ongoing experiment, a process in which you proceed by trial and error; and carefully choose your mentors. The boys had turned a little glassy-eyed at that point, and I wasn't sure they were tracking. They were probably thinking about the brownies and pies waiting for them after I finished talking.

"When I finished high school, I kept gradually improving," I said. "After my junior year in college, I never really changed my training. Consistency is the key. My senior year in college, I got second at the NCAA 2-Mile indoors, and that was when I thought I might have a future. But I never changed my approach."

It was time to talk a little bit about my friendship with Steve

Prefontaine. I knew that would perk up the young men, and I enjoyed providing some inside information about my late friend, and helping the kids feel more connected to his memory. "My mentor, after leaving college, was Steve Prefontaine. Steve and I would share the load in training. Then at a race we'd try to beat each other's brains out. As soon as we crossed the line, we switched it off and became friends again."

I returned to my favorite topic. I got specific with training advice. "The increase in your mileage goes to support your anaerobic conditioning," I said. "Do your intervals first, and let that training dictate how far you run to recover. Make your easy days very easy and your hard days very hard."

It was time to wrap it up. I had given the boys plenty to think about, maybe too much. I had tried to give them a preview of their running careers, a look ahead at the joys and hazards. My gold medal was a sign of all the things that could go right, and I gave them a hint—a taste—of the ways that running could go wrong.

I gave them so much to think about that they failed to notice the gap in my narrative; I had been so absorbed in the telling that I didn't notice it myself. I had talked about all my influences, my mentors famous and obscure, my coaches and fellow athletes, and bitter rivals and loyal training partners. True to form, however, I had breathed not a word about the person who, along with his mother, should be a boy's strongest and most enduring influence. I had not mentioned my father.

+ + +

I returned from Fort Wayne and called the writer. I said it was okay with me if he talked to my sisters. When he asked for contact information, however, there wasn't much I could give him. I had

had shockingly little contact with my sisters over the last 40 years. Fear and shame had kept us apart. On the rare occasions when we met, we never talked about our father or discussed what he'd done to us. His violence was always there, the elephant in the room, the reason we couldn't look each other in the eye, but we never talked about it.

Now I was changing the script, and I didn't know what to expect. Similar to our childhood beatings, I was more concerned about how the change would affect my siblings than the discomfort I was feeling myself. Would they remember the crimes more clearly than I had been able to? Would they be willing or able to talk about their suffering? The magazine was understandably concerned that I had exaggerated or even fabricated my father's crimes. I wasn't worried about that. I knew I was telling the truth. I worried that by going public I was forcing my siblings into confronting truths they might prefer to keep buried.

To my great relief, those worries proved unfounded. The reporter's invitation to comment opened floodgates for my sisters; it was as if they'd been waiting for decades to be asked these questions. To my surprise and outrage, however, the crimes they related were far more horrific and frequent than the ones I'd been able to summon. I don't see the purpose of recounting their testimony here. My sister Barbara, who now makes her living as a counselor for juveniles in the criminal justice system, summarized our childhood experience: "There is no question my father was a criminal," she told the writer. "If he were charged today for what he did to us then, he would go to prison, no question."

The story was published later in 2011. I was amazed and humbled by the number of readers who responded with stories of their own abusive childhoods. I decided that I wasn't going to present myself as an expert on the topic. I was not about to hit the lecture and talk-show circuit. For certain groups and individuals, however, I thought I had something to offer.

Most gratifying, instead of deepening our pain and widening the chasm separating us, the publication of the story, the airing of the truth, drew the surviving Shorter children closer together. We would never fully regain what our father had robbed from us, but now we could look each other in the eye.

I doubt that the girl in Springfield, Missouri—the battered and frightened young woman who confessed to me that my story was also her story—ever read the article. But I hope she's doing okay. Someday, if our paths cross again, I would like to thank her.

Epilogue

Even though I'm far too busy on race day to run it, even busier than I am at the Middletown 10-K or the Hood to Coast Relay, the Frank Shorter Race4 Kids' Health 5-K forms the most important event on my running calendar. April 2016 marked the eighth annual running. Held in Broomfield, a town close to Denver, the race draws runners hoping to qualify for the Bolder Boulder 10-K, the nation's second-largest road race, which Steve Bosley and I cofounded in 1979. The bulk of the Kids' Health 5-K field, however, consists of children and families who participate in the Healthy Learning Paths program through various elementary schools in the area.

The run starts and finishes in the 1stBank Center, a large indoor arena, where I spend a long and happy morning welcoming sponsors and donors, thanking volunteers, posing for smartphone snapshots with fans, giving interviews to the media, and meeting and greeting the children and families, especially the kids I had visited in classrooms and assemblies during the weeks leading up to the event.

Despite the demands and hectic pace, I find time to savor small moments and register certain details and individuals. I remember the burly, tattooed young Latino man and his decked-out wife who were there cheering on their little daughter as she completed the kids' fun run. By their obvious pleasure and amazement, I could tell that the parents were totally new to this type of health-and-fitness–themed event; exactly the audience that the Healthy Learning Paths program was hoping to reach. And, perhaps, the man's massive shoulders and hard-edged style reminded me of the guys who had chased me down the highway in New Mexico in 1972.

Along with the kids and adults new to the sport, the race draws plenty of experienced runners, middle- and upper-middle-class athletes wearing Lycra tights and expensive training shoes. Christine Marchioni, MD, a pediatrician and the co-race director and head of the Healthy Learning Paths program, reminds me that this crowd is just as key to the day's success and often just as needy of the program's message. "Your story proves that trouble can fall on kids from the most accomplished and affluent families," Chris says. "Everybody has scars."

And then there are the varsity football players from the University of Colorado, who get up at 5 a.m. and bus down from Boulder to mingle at the event in their game jerseys, cheer on the kids, and sign autographs—their appearance is always one of the day's biggest hits. At the end of the 2016 event, I took a moment to privately thank the players and to suggest that in their future careers they should always take the time to give back to their communities. When I finished my brief remarks, one of the players—a hulking 300-pounder—came up to me. His shy demeanor reminded me of the girl who had approached me after my talk in Springfield, Missouri, in 2011.

"Thank you for bringing me here today, sir," the kid said. "It really meant a lot to me. I'm not going to forget it."

+ + +

My involvement in the race and program began one day in 2008, at my house in Boulder on the edge of Wonderland Lake. It was late winter, but you could taste spring in the air. I was just back from my late-morning workout at the gym. It was the year of my father's death and my hip-resurfacing surgery. Both of those events were still a few months away, however, and my pain persisted.

The phone rang. It was Dr. Marchioni. "Please, call me Chris," she said, and started talking as if we were old acquaintances resuming a conversation broken off a few minutes earlier.

Chris explained that her program embedded health, fitness, and nutrition education into elementary school curriculums. The idea was to give kids solid information—give them the facts—and let them decide for themselves what to do with it. Because today, Chris continued, children couldn't rely on adults to set them on the path to a healthy life.

Instead, most often, the adult world points children in the opposite direction. They are insidiously and relentlessly bombarded by carefully targeted marketing and advertising from the corporate snack industry. Too often, their parents are distracted and disengaged. Chris had seen the result in her practice—fat kids, emotionally disturbed kids, 10-year-olds already suffering from adult-onset diabetes.

"Ten-year-olds!" she repeated. "When I was in medical school, not all that long ago, we learned it took a lifetime of bad habits to develop type 2 diabetes. And now in my office it is almost as common as the flu."

The situation was blasphemous, she felt, a crime that could so easily be prevented. So in 2005 Chris had stepped away from clinical practice to start Healthy Learning Paths, a program that was already up and running in several schools in the Denver metro area. She was calling to see if I might want to get involved, if I might have some ideas for the fitness component of the program, how to get kids moving . . .

Before replying, I asked how she had heard of me. She said she knew about the Olympic gold medal and that I had cofounded the Bolder Boulder 10-K. "I also understand that you care about fair play," Chris said. "You're active in the anti-doping movement."

Even over the phone, Dr. Marchioni's energy, commitment, and intelligence were almost palpable. I got the same vibe from her that I had gotten from Steve Bosley and the late Fred Lebow. Chris had a vision, and she also had a plan.

My feeling was confirmed when I met the doctor in person. A brisk, smart, cheerful woman, Chris was dead serious about her work but didn't take herself overly seriously. I thought about John Parker and those hard, golden interval-workout days with the Florida Track Club in Gainesville. On the track you tried to tear each other's throats out, and afterward you tore around town together on a motor scooter.

I also thought about Steve Prefontaine and the track meet at Hayward Field on the day that he died. I had accepted Pre's invitation to run in that unsanctioned competition because the cause was just and the timing felt right. By the same token, Dr. Marchioni's cause—empowering children, the issue that I had been consciously and unconsciously grappling with for my entire life—was just, the program was based in my home state of Colorado, and the timing was right: At this stage of my life and career, I had the power to help. I suggested to Chris that we put on a road race benefiting Healthy Learning Paths.

Dr. Marchioni took my idea and, well, ran with it. Together we organized the first edition of the Frank Shorter Race4 Kids' Health 5-K in April 2009. The run formed the focal point for a range of events and talks, reinforcing the values of physical activity and a healthy diet. The goal was to help families learn to filter the misinformation that the corporate culture kept ramming down their throats. The race proved a success, evolving into a major annual event on the local running calendar. In 2016 we drew 3,500 participants.

Chris's dedication and energy came as no surprise, but she was somewhat taken aback by the intensity of my commitment. She assumed that like most "personalities" supporting a cause, I would show up on race day and talk to the media and the power brokers at the cocktail parties. Like John Elway or Peyton Manning, the Denver Broncos quarterback heroes, I would confine my activities to grip-and-grins for the cameras. That would have been fine with Chris; that was all she expected from me. But I was willing—eager—to roll up my sleeves and interact with the kids, speaking often in their classrooms and at school assemblies.

In my talks I tried to convey a sense of safety and respect and always sought to be positive; I wanted to accurately model the Healthy Paths philosophy. I made it clear to the kids that they weren't being judged, manipulated, or pitched to; I wasn't trying to sell them a product. I knew that I appeared ancient to these schoolchildren—indeed, most of the grown-ups in their lives never would have heard of me. Would I be able to relate? Would the kids listen?

By way of introduction, I brought along a visual aid—a DVD clip of me running into the Munich Olympic Stadium at the end of my gold medal marathon. That got the kids' attention. They might not understand the marathon, or distance running, but an Olympic gold medal had an archetypal appeal. I have never taken my medal for granted. As many times as I've showed that clip, no matter the audience, I'm invariably impressed by the power of the Olympic ideal to transcend age, gender, nationality, and every other division or barrier. The gold medal is a responsibility that I take seriously. Despite the corruption and cynicism, the corporate lying and the state-sponsored doping, an Olympic gold medal still means something. It meant something to those kids, too.

So with the Olympic bond established, I was better able to relate to the children, to fashion that ineffable cone of safety. Mindful of the specifics of Chris's program, I stressed to the kids that they had the power to choose wisely and shut out the falsehoods; they didn't have to accept the labels that the grown-up world stuck on them.

I knew that Chris was grateful for my involvement—I never turned down one of her requests and, in fact, volunteered for even the humblest jobs. I also suspected that she was a little puzzled. I couldn't explain to her why the event was so important to me, at least not until 2011, when the third edition of the race came around. That was the year I decided to go public about my father's crimes and when the story appeared in *Runner's World*.

As the publication date approached, I called Chris and asked to meet her for coffee—a reversal of the normal protocol for our get-togethers. Intrigued by the invitation, she accepted at once. I was somewhat uncertain about the meeting. After I told her about my childhood abuse, about the beatings I had suffered from my father, would she still want to work with me? Had I turned into damaged goods? Would my past disqualify me from working with kids? Would Chris now suspect that I had my own agenda to promote?

We sat down with our coffee. I took a deep breath and launched into it. "Chris," I said, "I want to tell you the story before you read it in a magazine."

I proceeded to deliver a condensed version of the story I had told the *Runner's World* reporter: how I'd been abused as a child by my father, a respected physician who treated many of the children in our town. I didn't need to go into the details. As was the case with juvenile type 2 diabetes and other tragically unnecessary plagues, the evidence of parental abuse was something that Chris had seen almost daily in her practice. She recognized the song all too well.

"I thought you should know," I said in conclusion, "that if you decide you can't work with me any longer or if you want me to help in a different manner, I wouldn't argue."

Chris took a moment before responding. To my surprise, her eyes glistened with tears. She said that now she understood why I'd embraced a cause that, for many others in my position, would have been a vexing obligation or afterthought.

"Frank," she said, "this makes me want to work with you all the more."

I asked Chris her opinion on how I should approach the subject when I talked to kids. After another moment's thought, she suggested that I didn't have to discuss it explicitly.

"In a way, you've already been telling this story," she said. "You tell it when you make kids feel safe, when you respect them as individuals, and when they learn that even the strongest and most successful person has scars. When you do that, you're already telling your story."

Acknowledgments

Frank Shorter

Many thanks to John Brant. I feel grateful, happy, and blessed now that we have finished our collaboration. I asked for his help because, even though my manner has always been to focus on and work to enhance my strengths, I like to think I have also been careful to honestly recognize my limitations. I do not consider myself a writer.

When Kenny Moore and I first traveled overseas on the track circuit in 1969, I quickly realized he was a gifted writer and that I was, if anything, occupying the verbal half of our hotel room. That is why I asked John to help me express myself in words, and he has been incredibly true to the task. It is also why I asked Kenny Moore to write the foreword. Who better to bring the story full circle than the first close friend I made when I realized I might be competitive at the elite level?

Discovering that I loved to run literally saved me from my childhood and put me on a life path that still continues. Even as a child, I somehow knew I was fortunate simply to be alive. I went out the front door to celebrate my blessings through the running motion and so my journey began.

Along the way I looked for what I always instinctively felt were good people to emulate. As an adult my motto became "find the good people and keep them." These mentors, role models, and friends shaped and guided my life goals from an early age. I like to think they laid the foundation for how I decided to carry on after I had achieved the highest goal in my sport: winning the Olympic Marathon. Here are just a few I would like to thank. Many more will be thanked privately.

First, the Preston family in Middletown, New York. Dr. Alec Preston allowed me to experience what it was like to feel safe in a normal loving family environment. Mary Preston put me on the academic fast track that proved to be my escape route from home.

Richard Kellom, the Mount Hermon School ski coach who, somehow, listened and understood when I told him I was going to focus on running and left his team my senior year, even though I was the captain. He was the first adult to believe I was serious about my running goals.

Of course, at Yale there was Robert Giegengack who taught me how to coach myself. But there was also my roommate, Ken Davis. As with Kenny Moore with writing, four years later, I quickly realized that I was the academic underachiever, this time sharing a Yale college room. I truly believe that in the field of medicine, particularly in the chemical treatment of both schizophrenia and Alzheimer's disease, Ken's achievements have been monumental. The future Dr. Davis mentored and guided me through my premed studies and showed me how in both the academic and athletic worlds, consistent hard work and realistic goal setting can and should be partnered with innate intelligence or athletic ability: Don't waste the opportunity or squander your talent. I applied his work ethic to my training routine after graduation.

Don and Mary Gordon Roberts and her father, Al, who have contributed to our sport in ways beyond my means.

Jack Bacheler showed me by example how to fine tune and individualize my training when I first moved to Gainesville, Florida. At first he let me tag along. After three weeks he turned to me and said "You've lasted longer than anyone before." Two years later, in the Olympic Marathon, we were still running together.

Pre (he never minded my calling him Steve) and I qualified for our first international team on the same day in 1969. Just as with my friendship with Kenny Moore, I believe it was meant to be. He taught me to truly trust my training partner. When I think of him and how he died, I do something I seldom if ever do: I think about "what if?" I visualize him in a second chance Olympic Games 5,000 meter race. It was not meant to be.

Carl and Tony Ruzicka are fast and true friends from Yale, a couple of the good people who have always had my best interests at heart, financially and otherwise. They are not afraid to advise me, even in the toughest way, and I always trust their judgment.

Lawyers Joe French and Bob Stone gave me a part-time job when I was just out of law school so I could train. Joe was my first true friend in Boulder, and Bob actually composed the TAC Trust document that opened up all Olympic sports to prize money. I just did the typing.

Steve Bosley, my banker, became a very close friend, advisor, and co-worker in advancing running as a mass participation sport.

Shay and George Hirsch, kindred spirits in running. George as a running friend who also happened to publish *Runners World* and Shay, whose spirit and kindness toward me when I was very ill helped me become a believer.

My mother, Katherine, and my siblings, Susan, Nanette, Ruth, Chris, Mary, Amie, Barbara, and Michael. May you all continue to find more and more peace.

And most important, my children Alex, Mark and his partner, Cat, and Julie; granddaughters Adi and Kaela, their mother Kira, and partners Louise, Paddy, and Michelle.

Thank you all.

John Brant

As one of the multitude of Baby Boomers who were thrilled and inspired by Frank Shorter's gold-medal marathon run at the 1972 Munich Olympics, I feel honored to have helped Frank tell his story and grateful for the friendship we have forged over the course of writing this book. The grace and courage he demonstrated as an Olympian have again been on full display.

Thanks to our editor, Mark Weinstein, for his steadfast faith in this project, and his insightful guidance in its execution.

Thank you to Charlie Butler, David Willey, and John Atwood, the *Runner's World* editors who expertly directed the 2011 magazine story from which this book evolved.

Thank you to Frank Shorter's sisters and brothers, for all they endured, and all they have bravely shared.

Thank you to Patricia Gregorio, my wife, who inspires every good sentence that I write.

Index

An asterisk (*) indicates photos shown in photo inserts.

    father of *(cont.)*
        Frank's family and, visit of, 188
        at hometown celebration of
            Olympic gold medal, 123–25
        illness of, 187, 190
        Mount Hermon acceptance of
            Frank and, 26
        Yale acceptance of Frank and,
            34
    favorite workout of, 226
    Florida Track Club and, 66–68,
        70, 125–26
    Fort Wayne talk by, 223–30
    Franke's investigation of doping
        and, 204–6
    Ghost Ranch summer job of,
        40–41
    Giegengack and, 33, 36, 47, 63,
        74, 88, 118–19
    Gilliland and, 71, 84, 92, 125,
        128–29, 132, 147, 156–57,
        168
    grandparents of,* 6–7, 35
    Green and, 28–29
    guiding principle of, 12
    Hall (Warren) and, 28, 31
    Healthy Learning Paths program
        and, 233–39
    at Hollister's party, 136
    hometown celebration after
        Olympic medal win, 123–25
    injury of, 149–53, 175–76
    JFK assassination and, 30
    as law student, 71–73, 125–26, 128
    on Little League team*
    McCafferey and, 201, 204
    Marchioni and, 234–39
    as medical student, 35–37, 45,
        57–59
    memories of life and, 215–16, 221
    military hospital of birth visit by,
        xv
    at Montreal Olympic Games
        (1976), 158–67
    Moore (Kenny) and
        as competitors, 67, 73
        death of Prefontaine and,
            137–39

    friendship between, xv–xvi, 73,
        88, 134
    recover jog after Munich
        Olympic Marathon, 121
    training with, 67, 73
    Moscow Olympic Games (1980)
        and, 181
    mother of,* 6, 10, 15–16, 26, 44,
        50, 193
    at Mount Hermon School for
        boys,* 26–33
    move to New Mexico and,
        family's, 40–41
    Munich Massacre and, 103–8,
        226–28
    at Munich Olympic Games
        (1972),* xiii–xviii, 101–2,
        109–15, 227–28
    National Distance Running Hall
        of Fame induction of,*
    as NBC commentator, 188, 199
    Nike shoe sponsorship of, 141–43,
        160–63, 174
    1960s turbulence and, 42–43, 50
    1990s activities of, late, 199
    O'Keefe and, meeting, 41
    as Olympic gold medalist, 122–23
    Olympic ideal and, 237–38
    Paddy Shorter and, 183
    post-Olympic jobs of, 125, 188
    Prefontaine and
        death of Prefontaine and,
            137–39
        drive home from Hollister's
            party with, 136–37
        European barnstorm tour
            (1973–74) with, 128
        friendship between, 54, 229–30
        funeral service of Prefontaine
            and,* 139–40
        pacesetting and, 53–54
        personality differences
            between, 53
        survivor's guilt of Shorter and,
            139
        training similarities of, 53
        training with, 53–55, 67,
            129–33
    Preston family and, 12–13, 20, 36